My Hero Story, God's Glory

How To Overcome Betrayal, Delay, And Loss

DR. SHAWNISE CARTER

Walton Publishing House

Walton Publishing House
Weston, Florida
www.waltonpublishinghouse.com

Printed in the United States of America

Library of Congress Cataloging-in-Publication Data under

ISBN: 978-1-953993-83-0 (digital)
        978-1-953993-86-1 (paperback)

DEDICATION

I dedicate this book to my children. As you grow and experience life, I hope that you will learn to dance in the rain. Troubles come with the intent to shape you and not to break you. Perhaps one day you will be inclined to read this book and learn of the things that I have overcome with the help of God. Stumble but don't fall. Bend but don't break. Cry but don't lament. Be determined to get the very best out of life. Be prayerful, watchful, persistent, and know that you can live your dreams! I will always be here for you!

Table of Contents

The Foundation

My hero story includes lies, betrayal, deceit, victories, determination, faith, and laughter. Life has many ups and downs, twists and turns, gains and losses, and peaks and valleys. Through it all, there are lessons to be learned. It takes a mature, healed soul to look at life's trials and choose to see the message.

After 45 years of living, I am still learning about life and discovering myself. It took me almost two decades to realize that my pain had a purpose. Reflecting on my past experiences, I have learned that my setbacks were blessings in disguise. It is almost as if I gained more insight retrospectively.

Please understand that overcoming was not a quick process. I have had a lot of failures in life. For almost every aspiration I've had, there was an equal amount of failure. That indicates that my fear level was shallow, yet my expectation for success was very high. I have included some of my biggest failures in this book because I have gained the most knowledge from them. The stories within this book are only a small portion of the total number of times that I have failed.

The constant inner work it took to overcome those challenges revealed what I was made of. I always reverted to my spiritual foundation, the rock of my salvation. God's love for me never changed and never wavered. Although I faced humiliation, encountered temporary obstacles, and dealt with individuals who sought to undermine my success, God helped me overcome those challenges and I emerged as a hero!

If you have failed and want to begin again, you are in the right place. You may have failed once or multiple times, and you want to know how to keep going. I'm writing this book for you, the person who feels like all options have been exhausted. You feel like you have depleted all opportunities and you're unsure of your next steps.

Throughout the pages of this book, I will show you how to reconnect with yourself, recognize your haters, and latch onto your community, your motivators, and your cheerleaders. As you dive into my stories, I encourage you to reach out to a power higher than you to help you find the heroism in your story. Also included are suggestions, recommendations, and examples with Bible scriptures to confirm that you are not on this walk alone. I am reminded of the scripture in Philippians 1:6: *Being confident of this very thing, that He that has begun a good work in you will carry it on to completion until the day of Christ Jesus.*

I am the hero in my life, and by sharing my experiences, I hope it encourages you to tell your story. Everyone has a hero story!

Are you ready to overcome? Are you ready to win? If yes. Let's get started.

CHAPTER ONE

A Defining Moment

Working with children has always been a passion of mine. During my adolescence, babysitting was a common way for responsible and trustworthy teenagers to earn money. It was my first job. I provided babysitting services for a couple who were friends of my parents and had younger children. Whenever they wanted a "date night," they would ask my parents if I could watch their children for a few hours.

In my teenage years, children naturally gravitated towards me. Although I was a child myself, younger children often emulated me. As a child, you often want to be an adult or be older because you think that's where independence lies. Children appreciated the time I spent with them and thought that teenagers were the next best thing to being an adult.

I also worked with children in my church. I taught the primary classroom during Sunday school and other various activities. As life would have it, I have found myself teaching Sunday school again. The influence of these positive interactions ignited a passion for working with children. I knew I would either work with children or have many children one day. God blessed me to work with children for several years throughout my career and to have a big family!

MY ENTREPRENEURIAL JOURNEY

I have always wanted to be an entrepreneur. That was the most appealing option. No other setting attracted me in the same way that being a business owner did. While others had goals to graduate and work in the school setting as a speech-language pathologist, my sights were set on something else. As I listened to others delight in the epitome of what they imagined to be their clinical careers, the mere thought of not being independent caused me to feel restricted and prohibited, followed by the feeling of a lump being caught in my throat. I believed wholeheartedly that an entrepreneur was who God created me to be.

The drive for entrepreneurship came from within, fueled by a deep yearning to make a significant impact. My imagination was limitless, so why not aim for something grand? I was determined to achieve big things in my twenties and did not fear failure. It was either go big or go home.

A GREATER PURPOSE

When someone starts a business, they are often asked to define their "why." My focus was to instill the reality of business ownership in my child and future children. For me, there would be no better way to explain the value of hard work than to exemplify it. I wanted to build a legacy by providing a place for my children to learn the skills necessary to run a business successfully. My hope was for my children to grow up in my business. Witnessing the intricacies of entrepreneurship firsthand would have given them an advantage that others would have to pay to learn. That factor was of extreme importance. That was my "why."

I became an entrepreneur in 2006, starting as an independent contractor. That was a defining moment and the beginning of my experience as a business owner. I eventually opened a speech-language pathology private practice in 2009. I had plans to thrive in one location and then open several other places throughout my state and neighboring states.

I started with an 800 number instead of having a local area code because I wanted to prepare for a mass influx of clients. I'm going to date myself for a moment. In 2009, home phone plans included some area codes considered local calls and area codes deemed long-distance calls. The 800 number was a consideration for parents who did not have long-distance calling as part of their home phone plan. An 800 number was considered free and would be counted under the local minutes. Implementing measures like this was all a part of what I envisioned as my roadmap to success. What I thought would be the start of upward mobility with the stars as my finish line quickly turned into a series of events for which I was unprepared.

Upon starting my private practice, my concentrated population was adults. There was a void with adults receiving quality care for speech therapy services in a private practice setting, and my practice met the community's needs. It was essential to be in that place where other people (specifically African Americans) could observe a young business owner who looked like them.

Although my business plan was developed with adults being my targeted market, most of my caseload consisted of children under 18. God showed me that it wasn't time to work with adults yet. My purpose developed early on in life and was tied to working with children. Many are the plans in a person's heart, but it is the LORD's purpose that prevails. (Proverbs 19:21).

While working with children, I often encountered cases where they struggled with oral motor development. This presentation would usually be accompanied by paralysis or paresis, making it difficult for them to manage their oral secretions. To prevent bodily fluids from spilling on my clothes, I would typically wear scrubs and a lab jacket and would often alter my work wardrobe to include clothing items that were easily washable in case of any accidents. Although this was just part of the job, it became apparent one day when I left my office to run some errands that not everyone was familiar with my line of work. As I walked to the store next door, two young African American women who appeared to be in their early twenties were walking in simultaneously. Wearing my long white lab jacket, like those worn by physicians, I overheard one of them ask,

"Do you think that she's a doctor?"

The other girl responded, "Yeah, right."

They looked at each other, chuckled, and found the joke amusing. I wasn't bothered or offended by the remark. However, it saddened me that they weren't exposed to the various types of doctors outside medical physicians who wear lab jackets. They needed to be made aware of the multiple types of doctors, including allied health professionals and medical professionals who routinely wear lab jackets. Scientists wear white lab jackets. Dentists wear lab jackets. Physical therapists, nurses, occupational therapists, and speech therapists wear lab jackets. It is a very narrow scope of view to assume that only physicians wear lab jackets.

I was young, Black, wearing gym shoes, scrubs, and a lab jacket -*I couldn't have been a doctor.* That narrow way of thinking hurt me more than the joke ever could. At that moment, I had an epiphany. *Wow, is this why my business is here, in my community? My people need to see young, Black people owning businesses!* I thought.

From that moment, I realized my purpose was to serve the community and be the representation needed in that area. If the young women saw more African American professionals wearing lab jackets and owning businesses, it wouldn't be something to laugh about. It may not be a joke at all. And if someone made that joke, the other person would hopefully respond, "No, actually, that's not unreasonable to assume that she could be a physician."

I knew I had work to do until consciousness arrived at that level. There ensued my mission in the community. Helping and being a solution was the obvious thing. My primary assignment was always to help people, but the mission became to be that representation until the concept of young, Black medical and allied health professionals was no longer a foreign visual.

Although I started with my ambitions, my purpose was much bigger than that. Purpose has a way of showing up and changing our way of thinking. Looking back, I can see how my ambitions were the starting point for something more significant than myself.

Through my work, I was not only able to provide for my family financially, but I was also able to inspire and uplift others. Today, as I reflect on my journey, I realize that purpose is a powerful force that can transform our lives and the lives of those around us. It can shift our perspective and priorities and ultimately lead us to make meaningful contributions to the world.

REFLECTION

Think about a time when you realized a bigger purpose in your life.

- Were other people involved?
- If yes, who were they?
- Is there more than one experience that confirmed this?
- What did you discover?
- How did it make you feel?

Take some time to journal your responses. Reflect on that moment by making a memo of it. This can be written, you can create voice recordings, or other electronic methods of documentation. Don't limit yourself to pen and paper. This exercise aims to make you reflect and will serve as foundational information as we dive deeper in to purpose.

MY STORY OF BEING BETRAYED

Pain Births Purpose

Being in business wasn't always easy. There were so many things that I faced as an entrepreneur. My heart was always with the community, and I felt obligated to serve them. Coming from a place of compassion and not wanting to turn away clients, I was the practice that accepted state insurance when other businesses would not. At that time, even outpatient hospitals had stopped accepting patients who were insured by the state. When parents called to inquire, "Hey, you're on the list as a provider; do you accept state insurance? My child needs speech therapy." I could not turn them away.

Initially, I attempted to have a good caseload mix. I tried to have some private insurance patients, private pay clients, along with state insurance clients to offset the wait time for state insurance reimbursement. They were always reimbursed at a lower rate than private insurance companies. They also needed to pay more quickly, which created a financial deficit.

Ultimately, I ended up suffering financially. The state was six months in arrears and millions of dollars in debt. It was said that the state budget was misused, and there were misallocated funds. As a result, I was forced to close my business. I couldn't continue to see clients knowing that there would be a six-month gap before my company was reimbursed for services. I wasn't the only agency affected. Anyone who billed services through the state insurance had the same problem. Transportation companies that billed state insurance, speech therapy companies, occupational therapy companies, vision services, and just about any business that had clients with insurance were affected.

Most people who go into business are advised to save enough money to cover six months of bills. The savings should be enough to cover the mortgage, rent, and other monthly expenses in case things go array. I used every ounce of savings I had to keep the business afloat; after an eight-year run of working independently, in 2014, sadly, I had to close the doors.

Did I try other options before closing? The answer is 'yes'. I tried a multitude of things. During that time, I even partnered with other "professionals." I use the word "professionals" loosely because, as it turns out, they were not professional at all, but I'll get into that in a bit.

A STORY OF BETRAYAL

A family member was acquainted with a group of ladies looking to start a business in a field whose services complemented my service population. To try and help save my business, I agreed to meet with them, even though we were strangers. However, after a few meetings and business discussions, I felt they were trustworthy.

Together, we chose office space with a nice amount of square footage, allowing us to treat clients in our individual offices with a joint common area and a waiting room. We all kept our independent corporations and established a corporation together. Although we billed our clients under our separate businesses for the convenience of referrals, we incorporated a new company to offer multiple services under one roof. That was the attraction of partnering with other business owners.

In addition, it was convenient to split the rent for our business location. The business relationship started semi-professional. The relationship emerged based on our similar business aspirations, but there were some personality red flags. I didn't want to make too much out of it, so I chalked it up to us getting to know one another. On the outside, it seemed like a perfect fit. We would pray before every meeting. We were great at the collaboration and execution of ideas.

Somehow, things started to change, and the attitudes of my partners started to shift. Instead of being partners and looking out for each other, it began to become competitive. Competing was the farthest thing from my mind. I have tunnel vision in achieving my own goals, so it was easy to focus on my clients and share opportunities with my business partners when applicable.

By the time I looked up, tension was beginning to build. I have discernment. There were times when I would walk into a room and could tell that a conversation had just ended and I was the topic of it, and not in a good way. It wasn't a good feeling. I also started to notice things were being done out of their paranoia. For example, we had a VOIP line for the office. As calls came in, we agreed that all calls would be transferred to the individual who provided the service the caller was seeking. However, instead of transferring my calls, they "accidentally" conferenced calls so the business partner who answered the phone could listen in on the conversation. I believe this was an attempt to gather information and determine how many referrals I was receiving. They were concerned that their volume of referrals wasn't equivalent to mine, despite offering different services. Speech therapy always had more demand.

Our office suite had individual doors, none of which had personal locks. (I mention these details because of what transpired when I returned to the office). One weekend, I left my work laptop in the office. I was highly focused on not bringing my work life home and keeping the two separate to maintain a healthy balance. Although I wasn't working, my partners told me they would be there working over the weekend.

When I returned to the office that Monday, my partners looked at me like they had seen a ghost. I knew something was off but wasn't sure what it was until I entered my office. My laptop was missing! I wondered, *had our office been broken into?* I quickly tried to get to the bottom of my missing laptop. If the main door was locked, what could have happened? I asked if any of their items were missing, and they said "no" and fumbled to provide a rationale for my missing laptop. I was immediately overcome with disappointment as I realized the only logical conclusion was that they had stolen my laptop. I looked at them in utter disbelief. *Did they forget they told me they would be in the office over the weekend?*

I called the police to report the stolen computer. The officers confirmed what I already knew. After recapping the series of events with the officer, he pulled me aside to tell me that it was an inside job. No forced entry, no other items missing other than my laptop, and my business partners admitting to being the last ones in the office made it an open-and-shut case. My partners attempted a last-ditch effort to not look like "the world's dumbest criminals" in front of the officer and offered a theory of possibly leaving the suite door unlocked on their way out and an intruder coming in after they had left.

The officer offered advice on his way out, "Get rid of them!"

I agreed with the officer and informed our building managers that a police report had been filed. Later that evening, I took the initiative to put a lock on my office door. The following week became even more awkward, as my partners made sure to coordinate their presence in the office when I was not there. They would either arrive as I left or refrain from entering altogether. After two weeks, I decided to ask them to vacate and provided them with a five-day notice. They were upset when I requested them to leave, but their guilty conscience wouldn't allow them to stay. They were well aware of what they had done and reluctantly departed.

Their departure was far from peaceful. As they were leaving, they left me a clear message by forcefully kicking open my office door and breaking the lock I had recently installed. However, this act did not deter me in any way. It was amusing because there was nothing on my laptop that they could access which would hinder my ability to see clients. It did not impact my revenue or professionalism in the slightest.

My electronic patient files and billing software installed on the stolen equipment required passwords. It wasn't the kind of system that would allow you to reset your password easily. You needed the old password to request a new one, so the only people they screwed up were themselves. Everything was password protected. They would be out of business if they were petty thieves because they lacked a plan.

After I kicked out my good-for-nothing business partners, I remained in that location for three years without them. Subsequently, I entered a different business location as the sole business owner for another two years. I hired staff and personnel (mainly family). I needed trustworthy people because that debacle taught me to keep genuine people around me.

I had to weigh my options to see what made more sense. Did I want people around whom I knew I could trust? Did I want people who I knew would have my back and would not steal from me? Did I want people I knew were good for my business and had a good spirit and heart? Did I want people who loved people and loved the families that we served?

Or did I want to take a chance with someone I didn't know? Did I want to trust someone who may start okay and become jealous or envious? Did I want to risk encountering someone who may want to take what I had earned instead of earning it themselves? Needless to say, I chose to work with my family.

The truth is it's not always good to work with family. Sometimes, they will take advantage of you. They don't work as hard as someone who does not have that relationship with you and wants a job and understands that if they don't perform, they can get fired. Family will use that familial relationship until strict corporate policies are implemented. I didn't have to worry about this with my family members and I was grateful that they were there for me. As you may imagine, my last business encounter infuriated them. They wanted to do everything in their power to prevent something like that from happening again.

GIVE IT YOUR ALL

Now stop and think if you were running a business, and let's say 55% of your company was provided upfront, but you would not get paid for six months from today. How long would it take to go out of business? That was my struggle. As a business owner, I did a ton of networking. I attended different events to meet city officials and inquire about any money within that township or any budgeted money left for business owners. I became certified as a woman-owned business or WBE. I applied for government contracts and submitted requests for proposals (RFPs).

Although I applied for RFPs in need of the same services that my company provided, it was very competitive. Larger companies would outbid me in many cases. The multi-year contracts proved to have extremely tough requirements, causing my small business to contend with companies that employed anywhere from 0-500 people. They had a workforce and positive cash flow beyond what was accessible to me.

I tried to salvage my business. I utilized every resource known. The next step was to return to where it all started: independent school contracting. I split my time between performing contract work in the schools and working from my office. This involved working in a school setting a few days out of the week and seeing clients in my office on alternate days. Some evenings, I would see clients after working in the school setting during the day. If you are a business owner or have ever been one, I'm sure you can relate to wearing too many hats.

It was counterproductive because I could not be in so many places simultaneously. Yes, the school money was good, but even though I was an independent contractor, I still answered to someone else. Every moment I worked in the schools took time away from running my own business. At what point was I going to be 100% administrative in my business? I was shaking the tree to run and catch the leaves, only to go back and shake the tree again so that more leaves could fall. I was a one-woman show, wearing myself thin.

In addition to working day and night, administrative duties could not be neglected. The bread and butter of the business was negotiating contracts.

However, marketing the company, balancing a profit and loss sheet, and paying family members for the billing and clerical work took a lot of time. I needed two of me. I hired a few speech pathology assistants to help me treat clients.

This allowed me to supervise them a percentage of the time while freeing up time for administrative duties. As I began to expand, I would start a contract with the schools, perform good work, keep the contract, and then hand it off to another therapist I had hired. Since the school district was familiar with my quality of work, they knew that the person I brought in to fill the position would also perform quality work. I had to hire people who worked well with the schools' parents, students, and teachers.

There were pros and cons to everything. After a while, labor for contractors became a burden because contractors desired high hourly rates. As an employer, I did not provide health benefits. They were strictly 1099 contractors. A high hourly rate was the attraction of being a contractor.

THE FORMULA

Here's an example of how this worked. The business owner initiates the contract, then determines the percentage needed to replace themself in the contract with another contractor.

As a business owner, I had to make a profit. The negotiations became so steep that I would pay my employees before I paid myself. The reimbursement from the schools that came in regularly would go directly to the contractors, and I would take what was left over. This particular model I relied on for income was not financially sustainable, but at that time, it was the only option familiar to me.

Although this was a temporary way to earn money consistently, it only resolved some cash flow issues. For illustrative reasons, let's say $70 an hour is the rate I could charge the school district. If I were the contractor, I would profit the entire amount. I knew I could not pay above $45 an hour when I hired a contractor. Once I replaced myself in the contract, that left me with a $25-an-hour profit for a full-time contract. Schools get several days off. During summer break, those are hours we could not bill. All Christmas break, all spring break, and all holidays during the school year, including teacher institute days, were days that were not billable. There were weeks throughout the school year when no money came in.

MY STORY OF LOSS

My waiting room was filled with toys, language-building vocabulary cards, puzzles, and stimulating materials that were engaging for kids. My daughter loved spending time there more than going home. It was like an extra recess for her. I would pick her up from school and return to the office for a few hours to tie some things up for the evening, and I knew that she could preoccupy herself in the other room. She would play with different toys designed to stimulate the brain for learning. I loved that I provided the opportunity for her as a single mother. I knew that I was doing something to secure her future, which meant the world to me.

Client referrals were still coming in but it wasn't enough to get me out of red and back in black. The tough decision had to be made to dissolve my business at the end of my lease. This meant conversations were had with parents explaining my decision to close. New client referrals had to be routed to other businesses. I began to question my entire purpose.

Was I ever supposed to be a business owner? Did I try hard enough? Were there additional resources that I didn't take advantage of because I didn't know they existed?

It hurt because, again, this was the legacy that I wanted to show my daughter and pass on to my future children. I had dreams of giving her one of my locations to run as the business manager. Even better, if she wanted to go into allied health, she could have a turnkey business waiting for her once she obtained the proper education and licensing.

Was it easy walking away? No! I tried encouraging myself by saying, *'Hey, this struggle will only last a while. You'll get your feet back firmly planted on solid ground. You're just going to go somewhere and work there for a year and get back into entrepreneurship. You can put some money aside and be back in business soon.'*

PUSHING PAST THE PAIN

Before closing, I took all my earnings and invested them back into my business. With one income and no investors, I could not sustain my company for the length of time needed to become profitable again. There were times when I would trade cars with a family member to keep my car from getting repossessed. I remember parking my car in the garage. My garage was detached from my house and had to be entered by driving through an alley. I was under such financial duress that I would step on the bumper of my car to reach high enough to look out of the window in my garage. I feared a tow truck would be in the alley waiting to block me off and take my car.

I was so disappointed. It was as if all my hopes, dreams, goals, and aspirations meant nothing. I saw all those wonderful things being flushed down the drain. Gone. Sunken. Drowned. My once thriving business was closing. It was hard to remain hopeful.

Storage unit with the remainder of my office equipment

As I looked around my office space, memories came flooding back. I remembered a few times when my daughter answered the phone at my office. She thought that the name of my business was "Adveesement." She answered the phone in her chipmunk voice using speech that was not fully phonetically developed and stated, "Adveesement Therapy. How can I help you?" I was mortified, but at the same time, it was so hilarious. She imitated what she heard and saw me do over and over again. I wanted her to remember that experience for years to come. I wanted her to have that moment and so many others like it for life.

I was so afraid that she would be so young and would forget all her mom's accomplishments. It was so crucial for me to make my child proud of me. Do you know how parents are proud of their children? I knew I was doing something big, and although she was too young to realize it, I wanted it to be a part of her fabric. In contrast, business ownership may have been a distant concept for some people. I wanted her to only be accustomed to business ownership.

I gave away a lot of furniture, took some learning materials and toys with me, and moved the rest of the furniture into storage.

LIFE IS A LESSON

My process of healing took years. I invested big and lost big! I lost my house and my car and eventually had to move back in with my parents. I cried a lot! There were several nights that I cried myself to sleep. I prayed in the moments when I had the strength to do so. When I didn't, I just said something quick and simple like, "God, I need you." Many times, I asked my mom to pray for and with me. I would cry in church every Sunday. I cried because I was mourning the loss of what I felt was my purpose in life. I didn't know what my next move should be. The planner in me didn't know how to relinquish control and let God lead, even if I didn't know where He was leading me.

Giving myself permission to acknowledge and process these emotions was crucial in reaching a point of acceptance. I could only break free from believing I was a failure by addressing and reconciling these feelings. This process took a while, as many questions arose during that time. Relying heavily on my support circle, I sought individuals who could help me navigate that chapter in life. My most prominent sources of support were my mom and dad, who continuously expressed their pride in me. They were extremely proud of what I had accomplished within that timeframe. While I believed they meant their words, I still believed that I was a failure.

OVERCOMING DEVASTATION

The fighter in me would not let me stay in that dark place. My first instinct was survival. I needed a source of income to provide for my daughter and me. It was essential to start over, beginning with the necessities of life. I started looking for a steady income (a salaried job) that included health benefits for my daughter and me.

Next, I had to establish a budget to determine my fixed and variable expenses vs. the income needed and decrease my variable costs. Once those were in place, I contacted my creditors and set up payment arrangements to take care of the debt that was incurred.

WHERE YOU ARE NOW IS NOT WHERE YOU WILL FINISH

What if I told you that failure is a part of success? Would you believe me? When we imagine ourselves having an impact, we often start from an area of passion. Wherever that place is, whether you want to open a beauty salon, a barber shop, a clothing boutique, a dental practice, a cafe, or start your line of natural hair products, you have a mental idea of what success looks like to you.

There was a version of success that I had envisioned and now I understand my process needed to include the hard lessons. Thankfully I had people who continued to speak life into me even when I wanted to give up. Although I wasn't always open to receiving their words, they always had my best interest in mind. Often, I would hear the words, "I would like you to know that you're not doing anything wrong." Whenever I heard those words, I would immediately become irritated. As an entrepreneur, hearing mentors tell me that "I'm not doing anything wrong" and having my bank account balance show up as 'all the way wrong' made me feel like I was definitely doing something wrong. Now that I have experience under my belt, I can advise that, if you have done everything within your capacity to build, but instead of advancing, you seem to decline, remain there, and wait for guidance.

If you have ever envisioned yourself being successful to the point where you're ready to start your own business, get out there and incorporate your company, start marketing to get clients, start working on products, and research investment opportunities. For most people, entrepreneurship doesn't come as a surprise.

GET HELP!

As a business owner, you need help to do everything. The goal is to continuously learn, do, and teach. Master the skills. Do well enough to teach it. Train your employees so they can replace your work and occupy the spaces where you once were. This will allow you to concentrate on more administrative tasks and delegate so that responsibilities are shared. This next section is to provide ideas for entrepreneurs. Try any or all of these suggestions. It may make a world of difference for you.

RESOURCES FOR ENTREPRENEURS

The Small Business Administration (SBA) has local offices throughout several states. A listing of your local office can be found by visiting this website- https://www.sba.gov/local-assistance/find?type=Community%20Navigator&address=46321&pageNumber=1

The local SBA office in my area is called the Service Corps of Retired Executives (SCORE). Another facility that helps small business owners is the Women's Business Center (WBC). You can search by zip code for the location nearest you by visiting this website- https://www.sba.gov/local-assistance/find?type=Women%E2%80%99s%20Business%20Center&pageNumber=1

The Women's Business Development Center (WBDC) and the Chamber of Commerce offer various funding options and microloans. The Chamber of Commerce has several programs designated by race and location (i.e., Chicago Chamber of Commerce, Hispanic Chamber of Commerce, Black Chamber of Commerce). Also, it is essential to note they are not exclusive to race only, meaning I was able to enroll and benefit from programs at the Hispanic Chamber of Commerce, although I am not of Latin descent.

If you are in business and thinking about retiring or profiting from one business and using those funds to invest in another business venture, you can position your business to be acquired by a larger company. I met with a larger therapy contract company and pitched my business to have them buy it out. Some business owners put money into an entity for a financial return and have had success repeating this same business model. This is considered **buyer entrepreneurship.**[1]

---

[1] Flori Needle, The Eight Types of Entrepreneurship, February 1st, 2021, https://blog.hubspot.com/sales/types-of-entrepreneurship

REFLECTION

Regardless of whether you initially identify with my story, I hope you will gradually find yourself relating to topics as if I am offering insight into your life. I hope the explanation provided created a sense of immersion as if you were an observer during the most transformative moments of my life. By sharing my experience of overcoming a failed business venture, I aim to equip you with the necessary tools to break free from your current stagnant situation and emerge stronger. Ultimately, I want you to meet the version of yourself beyond challenging circumstances.

- Have you ever had a story of betrayal in your life?
- This may seem like an unlikely follow-up question, but how did it help you?
- What did you learn from it?
- What did you learn about yourself?
- Have you ever pursued your dreams and fallen short?
- How did it make you feel?
- What series of emotions did you experience?
- How did you overcome the situation?

Please document these questions and your responses to them.

CHAPTER THREE

Your Innate Ability to Overcome: The Winner Within

I am so excited to start this next chapter with you. What does, "Your innate ability to overcome," mean to you? Think about your life for a moment. How would you describe yourself? What do you see in your inner-reflection? You are made in God's image and God's likeness. Can you see the overcomer inside of you?

Let's go a bit deeper. How do you define a win? What does your version of a win look like? I believe that everyone has a champion inside of them. We can face certain situations in life that prompt us to recognize the greatness inside of us. Your body's natural response to unfamiliar situations is fight or flight. When you choose to fight, you choose to utilize your innate ability to win. When you choose to fight, you ignite the champion inside.

IT IS IN MY DNA

Once I reflected on my experiences, I realized why entrepreneurship was so important to me. It was because it was in my genealogical makeup. It was who God designed me to be. When I began to look into my family history, I could name family members who owned real estate, funeral homes, a senior building, and a grandmother who was a nurse but also had a salon in her basement. All these things make me who I am.

An old proverb says, 'You don't know where you're going until you know where you came from.' That is a very true statement. When you are ready to give up because you've gone through situations that were so devastating that you would rather avoid them than try again, knowing where you come from can add substance. Tests in life can be so arduous that they cause an individual to question the very essence of who they thought they were. After challenges, some people redefine who they are or who they thought they were. It's important to understand where you come from and connect with those people who can relate to the things that you've gone through. These individuals can be your mentors and part of the community that encourages you through this time.

DEFEATING LOSSES

There was a time when I was ashamed that I had failed as a business owner. I felt that I let down so many people that were counting on me. The shame kept me afraid to leave the house, celebrate with others, or attend family events. You must change your focus if you are dealing with emotions of failure, shame, and humiliation. Concentrate on the truth of who God says you are and what you can accomplish through Him.

Although I had people around me telling me how well I did and that I was not a failure and should look at my accomplishments and be proud, I still felt that I didn't accomplish enough. If you need to believe it for yourself, though you may value other people's opinions of you, start the internal work. Clear your mental space of every harmful emotion and every negative experience. It's very much like flying on a plane. You are instructed to put on your oxygen mask first before you offer assistance to anyone around you. It is vital to get to a better place for yourself before you can be that person that helps others.

If you speak to anyone who has overcome tribulations, you will quickly learn they've been through some struggles. On the surface, you may view them as successful based on their wins. The reality is losses come with the territory. Everyone has been subjected to defeat. You may find solace in knowing that other people have been through difficult situations, but they persevered. Having a conversation and being vulnerable will allow you to discover that many victors have similar stories. Sharing these moments also encourages you to continue to strive towards your goals.

Despite setbacks and disappointments, an unwavering determination drives me forward. Here's my philosophy, 'I'm too brilliant to not be a millionaire.' I use this powerful mindset to motivate,

> **"I'm too brilliant to not be a millionaire."**

strengthen, and push through challenges. Even though losses hurt, something inside of you must make you dogmatic.

WINNER MENTALITY

A spiritual connection to God is the center of everything in life. God is the creator. When you are off balance spiritually, it impacts every area. I spend much time edifying and affirming myself in what God says about me. Some of my favorite scriptures include,

Yet in all these things we are more than conquerors through Him who loved us (Romans 8:37).

Her children arise and call her blessed; her husband also, and he praises her. Many women do noble things, but you surpass them all (Proverbs 31:28-29).

Greater is He that is within me, than He that is in the world (I John 4:4).

I can do all things through Christ, who strengthens me (Philippians 4:13).

Our beliefs, affirmations, and declarations must be spoken and demonstrated constantly. When you are at a point where you are so low and physically worn out, it is difficult for you to get up and try again, keep going. Whatever that thing was that failed you, push past it. Whatever you gave your all to and it was devastating, don't allow it to paralyze you. You can love again. Whatever brought you shame, you must forgive yourself to arrive where you are mentally, physically, and spiritually able to try it AGAIN!! Don't let your past mistakes have dominion over you. God gives us the power to have dominion over the things of this world.

YOUR INNATE ABILITY TO WIN

Unraveling Counterproductive Patterns and Overcoming Self-Sabotage

Think about where difficulties lie in your life. Take some time to conduct an honest self-reflection. Don't be discouraged by what you have experienced. There are benefits to journaling to help you sort through your feelings. This was very important and helpful for me as I processed my healing.

Reflection prompt #1. Revisit the moment when things started to spiral downward. It may be a tough place to recount emotionally, but it will provide so much insight. After you have identified those problematic areas and written them down, determine the themes. Were there behaviors that recurred throughout those moments? Were situations presented differently, but the underlying themes were the same? Put a name to it. Associate the behavior with a name. These counterproductive patterns are habits you don't want to repeat.

SELF-SABOTAGE

Let's discuss self-sabotage for a moment. As I reflected on my experience, I was able to identify my self-sabotaging behaviors.

- Some self-sabotaging behaviors include lack of faith.

- Self-doubt is another sabotage. Have you ever lacked belief in yourself or your ability to achieve success beyond a certain level?

- Another culprit of self-sabotage is pride. When you reflect on your goals, is there a certain point, you refused help from others and tried to do everything on your own?

- Naivety is another behavior. Perhaps, at one point, you were too trusting of other individuals who did not have your best interest in mind. This was one of my self-sabotaging behaviors. I was naive and too trusting of people that I did not know. The last thing you should do is get to know people you are unfamiliar with while simultaneously running a business with them. It is difficult for best friends to go into business with each other. Indeed, there's some level of difficulty that perfect strangers will experience.

- The pesky repeat offender of impunctuality is also a natural deterrent. You frequently ran late to engagements and meetings or did not keep calendar appointments.

- Another behavior often overlooked is not investing in yourself. You may not have accessed resources for a business owner. You could have been inexperienced. You didn't know what you didn't know. So, you didn't educate yourself and take the time to invest in yourself as a business owner.

- Another self-sabotaging behavior is avoidance. There are some situations people avoid because they do not want to fail. It's not uncommon to play it safe because you did not want to be disappointed with the outcome.

- Another counterproductive behavior was not following a business and financial plan. I had a business plan, but it was just something I established and stuck in a file. I never referenced it for guidance. I often completed a profit and loss sheet at the end of the year for tax purposes but did not balance it weekly or even month by month. This exposed my finances wholly, and an accurate financial plan was never developed. I knew that money was tight, and other than trying to get more clients and hire more therapists to see the clients, I had no actual financial goals.

Now that you have reviewed this section, think about your situation. What role did counterproductive behaviors play in the demise of your attempted goal?

SOLUTIONS FOR THE COUNTERPRODUCTIVE CYCLE

Once you begin to look at those different experiences and identify self-sabotaging behaviors, the next step is to devise a plan. How could you approach situations differently? Hindsight is 20/20. Use your reflection to gain perspective and identify how you succumbed to unfavorable circumstances. The easiest way to achieve different results is by doing something different. If you don't like the outcome, change the action. The next time you face a similar circumstance, change your behavior. Figure out a plan to recognize its demise before it happens and pivot accordingly. This will ensure a different outcome.

Let me explain this in a simple example. If you chronically run late, leave earlier to allow yourself more time. Pick out your wardrobe the night before. Set your alarm to get up earlier. If it is your first time driving to a new location, map out the route by going there the day before so that you become familiar with the route. There are solutions to the bad habits that we develop.

You don't have to fall victim to the exact situations repeatedly. The previous paragraph gave an example like it's a one-and-done. That is not true for everyone. What if you struggle with pride and don't ask for help because you don't want to appear needy or vulnerable? Be honest about how much help you will need to overcome this situation. This doesn't have to be cyclical if you can identify triggers.

ADDRESSING TOXIC BEHAVIORS

Let's explore why counterproductive behaviors must be reconciled before moving into your future. Toxic behaviors must be addressed for positive change to take place. The first step in recovery is acceptance. If you don't take the time to write about your life, you can miss silent behaviors. If negative people are somehow drawn to you, all that toxic bitterness is transferred to you. If people who possess these traits attach themselves to you, there's a reason why they are attracted to you. This will require self-assessment to determine why these people consider being in your company common ground. Are you emoting in a way that feels familiar to them? Is there something within you that overly dramatic people can identify with and, therefore, feel comfortable dumping on you during a crisis or a situation? It could be that you're a good listener, or maybe it's time to do some self-introspection.

Catering to business of no consequence to you is a silent time waster. As much as you want to be there for people, some need help from trained professionals. There's a balance between being a good friend and being unnecessarily dragged into the drama of others. Set boundaries. Determine when you want to be bothered by certain people, especially if you're not in a good space. Hearing someone else's issues will drag you down. Don't answer the phone. Identification of these behaviors as well as your role in them is important. You don't want to continue to repeat the same venomous cycles.

Here are some simple solutions to dealing with "dramatic" friends or family.

- Call them when you have 10 minutes to spare because you are going into a store or to an activity. This way, you get that phone conversation in, check their well-being, and don't waste time wallowing in their pity or whatever they are trying to pull you into.

If **you** are the person who likes to throw the pity party

- Don't focus on everything that went wrong. Continue to make goals for yourself. When you constantly reach for that next thing, you don't have time to focus on what's not working and what you lack.

- Implement tunnel vision to replace those negative behaviors with positive, productive behaviors. Switch your focus to more positive things.

- Keep track of daily accomplishments without being distracted or ineffective. If this means creating a vision board, do it. List things that you can see yourself accomplishing. You don't have to do it all on your own. You can set the goal and ask God to provide you with everything. He will send the resources you need.

- Place the vision board in a room you frequent so that you can constantly grab inspiration from it. Put scriptures up so that you can profess them. Hang decor you created or purchased with inspirational sayings so you can absorb them in your system.

- Store daily reminders on your phone to speak these positive things into existence. The goal is to stay focused on what it is that you have been tasked with the responsibility of accomplishing.

Reflection prompt #2. Identify the character traits you exhibit in certain situations. Are those character traits positive things that you want to continue? Or are those character traits things that you don't necessarily like? How can you improve those areas?

MY STORY OF DELAY

UNVEILING THE POWER WITHIN TO OVERCOME OBSTACLES

I recall a time when I faced a disappointing life experience while enrolled in a doctoral program. Initially, I was excited when I decided to pursue my doctoral degree. I even encouraged my friends to embark on this journey with me regardless of their field. Back then, hybrid programs were still relatively new, with some classmates attending in-person while others were virtual.

At first, everything went smoothly, even though it had been six years since I was last enrolled in a degree program, and the online format was unfamiliar. Each professor had a unique way of organizing assignments, projects, and discussions. Unfortunately, I missed an entire section of classwork due to this unfamiliarity. Realizing my mistake, I reached out to my professor, only to discover that she had to leave mid-semester due to health reasons. The incoming professor was there as damage control, unable to access any work that had previously been submitted. Consequently, I failed that class but retook it later, receiving an A. Since I retook the course, the initial grade was stricken from my grade point average (GPA).

Undeterred, I continued the program, earning straight A's and completing 30 credit hours with a cumulative 4.0 GPA. After three uneventful years, with only three classes and my dissertation remaining to meet the graduation criteria, I encountered a devastating situation. I became the target of a professor with a personal vendetta against me. Although it was difficult to prove, it became apparent that this decision was racially charged, as systemic racism in academia can often be covert. When an instructor says, 'You don't display mastery in your writing' but cannot express what hasn't been mastered, it becomes their word against yours.

Ultimately, the professor assigned the final grade and, in my case, gave any point value necessary to make sure that I didn't pass her class. I believe she intentionally held onto the two assignments worth the most points until two days before the end of the grading period, even though the assignment due dates were weeks apart from each other.

I remember her phone call like it was yesterday,

"Shawnise, you don't display mastery in your writing. If you don't correct this, I'm going to have to fail you."

I had just left a patient's house and was racing down the expressway to treat my next patient.

I immediately thought, *who have I wronged, and how do I make it right? What have I done to deserve this, and what form of payback is this?* The thoughts in my head were circulating faster than I was driving. I managed to blurt out, "Please explain what I haven't mastered and what is lacking?"

"Your writing includes a lot of work that isn't yours," she spoke.

"It's a research paper on your assigned topic, so much of the information is not my work. I've paraphrased and cited every source that I used in my paper. Are you saying that my work is plagiarized?" I asked.

"No. You will not pass my class if you don't correct this, and you only have two days before the semester ends. I don't know what you're going to do."

At this point, I realized that passing me was not her goal. *Is she receiving pleasure from this? Have I been targeted? Is this racism?* I had to ask myself a question that is all too familiar to a person of color: would I be receiving this call if I were White?

"How can I fix my errors? Will you be returning my papers with feedback?" I asked.

"No. I will wait until you resubmit your papers to grade them," she answered.

"Just to confirm, you would like me to rewrite my papers without guidance on what needs to be improved?"

"Yes," She answered firmly.

My worry turned into fear. "I will be at risk of being placed on academic probation, which will result in academic dismissal from the university if I don't pass your class. I only have three more classes to take, and I will have completed all coursework." I stated.

Feeling trapped and fearing expulsion from the program, I explored all possible avenues for redemption. I considered the rubrics in place to protect students, but even assigning points was subjective. Seeking guidance, I turned to the writing center, hastily submitting my papers for review. Their feedback confirmed that my papers were well-written and scholarly, without any traces of plagiarism.

With a mix of uncertainty and hope, I resubmitted my papers to the professor, only for my worst nightmare to come true. She gave me a score two points below a passing grade, resulting in academic dismissal. Determined for this to not be the end of my academic experience, I appealed her decision, but the committee proved ruthless. They even failed to attend our scheduled virtual hearing, with not so much as an apology the following day.

Despite being given the chance to appeal, it was evident that the process was not designed to be fair. The committee sided in favor of the professor, stating they could not overturn an assigned grade.

The experience was harrowing, abruptly halting my progress. My 4.0 GPA became a 3.8 GPA, and my 30 credit hours of doctoral coursework tarnished. Unbeknownst to me at the time, the university had a history of dismissing students of color and had faced multiple discrimination lawsuits. Although my case lacked overt evidence, I sought legal advice from an attorney familiar with the university's practices. I sought him out by examining court records of litigation against the university. He was listed as the student's lawyer in previous cases.

He agreed that I had a case because he had represented students who sued the university before for discrimination. "They say that you have a right to appeal your letter grade. They didn't say that the process would be fair," he told me. He burned with fury as he went on explaining how he would love to take my case. Unfortunately, my financial constraints at the time prevented me from retaining him.

Years later, attending a virtual town hall meeting on systemic racism in higher education, I discovered that many others had experienced similar situations. Hearing their stories, which mirrored my own, opened my eyes to the prevalence of this issue for people of color in academia. It instilled disdain and mistrust that initially deterred me from reapplying to other programs despite my determination to complete my doctoral degree.

I had to confront my triggers, change my behavior, and resolve that this professor's hatred and racist views would not hinder me from achieving my doctorate. It was an internal journey of self-work, learning to trust

God and believing that He selected me to go through this experience because He knew it would not break me. I prayed that God would allow this situation to make me resilient so that I could persevere.

When you ask something from God, He will often request something of you. He bade me to ask for forgiveness from the professor, who singled me out. Yes, that's correct. Initially, my response was, "Ask for forgiveness from someone who wronged me? She should be the one asking for my forgiveness." However, God knew that I was harboring resentment. He knew that those emotions had me in bondage and fear of moving forward. God knew that the onus was no longer on me if I asked for forgiveness. God could not bless me in academics until I released those unhealthy emotions.

It took a few years until I was in a place where I was no longer emotionally triggered by this trauma. I had to heal and really be ready to move forward without harboring ill will. I was mad at the university for condoning racist practices. I was mad at the professor for operating without consciousness. I was mad for my classmates who were also being singled out because they were Black. I was mad at the professor's colleagues who sat complicit and decided to not get involved. I was mad that they were not allies when I asked for letters of support. I was mad for the students who didn't know the university operated in this way and would be the next ones to fall victim to these unfortunate circumstances. I had to surrender those negative emotions, even though they were valid. I did not want bitterness to take root. Forward movement happened when I allowed God's light to cast out all the darkness looming from that experience.

Taking my power back, I made the call and spoke with her over the phone. She sat quietly and listened to everything that I said. I reminded her of who I was, when I had taken her class, the grade she gave me, and the fact that I appealed and was still dismissed from the university. I recall saying, "If I did anything to warrant your determination, I ask for your forgiveness." I waited for a returned request for forgiveness or an apology. It never happened. She did not say anything. She didn't act surprised to receive the call. Deciphering her thoughts or feelings was hard as she sat silently on the other end. To break the awkwardness of the moment, I told her that was the only reason for my call. Since the communication exchange was one-sided, I ended the call allowing her to return to her day.

After the call, I felt better. The load wasn't lifted immediately, but I felt closure. I knew that I did what was required of me. I knew that it was meant for it to happen at that time because she answered the phone, and I was not sent to her voicemail. I knew that she heard everything that I said. Determined to succeed but still not having clear insight on my next steps, I stopped and waited for God to reveal them.

Approximately eight years after making this call and ten years after my dismissal from the university, I mustered the courage to apply to a different, reputable doctoral program. Surprisingly, the professor who failed me at the other institution taught three classes at my new college. This led to a divine encounter with one of the committee members who reviewed student applications for acceptance into the program.

He called to let me know that I was accepted into the program. He also mentioned, upon review of my transcripts, he noticed that I had history with the same infamous professor. To summarize the conversation, he wanted me to know that she taught three classes at this university as well. He wasn't sure of the status of the current relationship (between the professor and I) but wanted to give a forewarning to see if being made aware of her involvement at this institution impacted my decision to attend the program.

I had to chuckle silently on the other end of the phone. I knew this was God making provision for me. In what world does a committee member provide personal calls to incoming students? This was not a formality to which I was accustomed. It showed me that he was aware of the situation and would be watching my progress should I decide to enroll. Sometimes, you must laugh at how God orchestrates things to work in your favor. You will never know what God has in store for you until you make the decision to move forward.

My response was, "I thank you for this call and your integrity. I will not allow anyone to stop me from earning my doctoral degree." After making that declaration, I enrolled in the upcoming semester. This time, I passed all three of her courses with all A's, encountering no issues, and she seemed to have no recollection of our past.

During my doctoral journey, God made even more provisions. He provided finances for me to pay tuition in the most unconventional ways through my husband. My husband was my biggest supporter and provided the encouragement that I needed every step of the way. He protected me. He covered me spiritually. I knew that I was never alone and never uncovered. Finally, four years later, I proudly graduated with my doctoral degree.

Was the situation that I experienced on the path to earning my doctoral degree fair? Absolutely not. It was a blessing that was delayed. It was undoubtedly hurtful and caused me to question my self-worth, purpose, and capabilities. However, I realized it did not attack my ability to gain knowledge. The fact that the same professor awarded me three A's and the only thing that changed was the university proved that my writing and intellect were not to blame. She had been allowed to act unjustly at the previous institution, whereas the new university upheld her to higher standards.

These Bible scriptures helped me make more sense of the entire situation.

- "Lord, how often shall my brother sin against me, and I forgive him? Up to seven times?" Jesus said to him, "I do not say to you, up to seven times, but up to seventy times seven." Matthew 18:21b-22

- For observe this very thing that you sorrowed in a godly manner: What diligence it produced in you, what clearing of yourselves, what indignation, what fear, what vehement desire, what zeal, what vindication! In all things, you proved yourselves to be clear in this matter. 2 Corinthians 7:11

- The Lord is my shepherd, I lack nothing. He makes me lie down in green pastures, He leads me beside quiet waters, He refreshes my soul. He guides me along the right paths for his name's sake. Even though I walk through the darkest valley, I will fear no evil, for you are with me; your rod and your staff, they comfort me. You prepare a table before me in the presence of my enemies. You anoint my head with oil; my cup overflows. Surely your goodness and love will follow me all the days of my life, and I will dwell in the house of the Lord forever. Psalm 23:1-6

Throughout my journey, I discovered the power within me to overcome obstacles and triumph over adversity. I realized that setbacks do not define my worth or determine my future. Instead, they serve as opportunities for growth and self-reflection. In adversity, I learned to embrace my strengths and capabilities, refusing to let others' biases and prejudices hold me back. I surrounded myself with a supportive network of mentors, friends, and family who believed in my potential and encouraged me to keep pushing forward.

I also sought solace in communities of individuals who had experienced similar academic challenges. Sharing our stories and supporting one another reminded me that I was not alone in this struggle. We empowered each other to rise above the barriers and create change within the academic landscape. Ultimately, my journey toward earning my doctoral degree was not just about the knowledge I gained in my field of study. It was a testament to my resilience, determination, and faith in God. I discovered that success is not solely measured by grades or degrees but by the strength of character and the ability to overcome adversity.

Today, I stand proudly as a doctoral degree holder, not allowing past experiences to define or limit my potential. I continue to advocate for equity and inclusion in education, using my voice and experiences to create a more just and fairer academic environment for all.

In sharing my story, I hope to inspire others who may have faced similar challenges or have been discouraged by setbacks. Remember, your worth and potential are not determined by the obstacles you face but by your resilience and determination to overcome them. Triumphing over adversity is not an easy journey but a transformative one. Through these challenges, we discover our true strength, resilience, and the power of God that works within us to overcome any obstacle that comes our way!

Let's focus on your innate ability to win!

REFLECTION

- What challenges have you faced, and how have you overcome them?

- How have setbacks and obstacles shaped your character and contributed to your inner winner?

- Who are the supportive individuals who have believed in your potential and encouraged you during challenging times? How have they made a difference in your journey?

- In what ways have you sought out communities or networks of individuals who have faced similar challenges? How have these connections helped you navigate adversity?

- Reflect on a time when you felt discouraged or doubted your abilities. How did you find the strength to persevere and continue pursuing your goals?

- How has your experience of triumphing over adversity influenced your perspective on success and resilience?

- What steps can you take to advocate for equity and inclusion, using your voice and experiences to create positive change?

- How can you support others who may be facing similar challenges or setbacks?

- What strategies or mindset shifts can you adopt to embrace your strengths and capabilities, regardless of others' biases or prejudices?

CHAPTER FOUR

The Genetic Makeup of a Champion

This chapter will delve into the profound concept of embracing your inner strength and purpose. We will explore how understanding and nurturing these aspects of yourself can contribute to personal growth, fulfillment, and a sense of direction in life. By tapping into your inner strength and aligning with your purpose, you can unlock your full potential and live a more purposeful and meaningful life.

As a foundation to your success, first start with identifying your gifts. Once identified you will leverage them as assets to help you win in life. Your gifts are things that come quickly to you that other people must work hard to achieve. Another way to identify your gifts is to identify the areas in your life that are constantly being attacked. This may be an area where God wants to do something more prominent in your life and the enemy knows this, so he wants to stop you. The Bible tells us that they enemy goes around like a roaring lion, and he seeks to kill, steal, and destroy. You must be aware of the deceit that the enemy may try to use to take from you or get you to stop operating in your gift so that you never realize the full potential of who you are in God.

To identify your gifts, go a step further and take note of the skills and talents that are common in your family. Ask surviving relatives what unique gifts are dominant in the family. Learn more about your ancestry if you are unaware. Ancestry DNA, 23andMe, or MyHeritage are good places to discover your rich family history. We all have a story. Test results can reveal things you may not know about your bloodline. It can help you take pride in who you are.

CHARACTERISTICS OF A WINNER

There are specific characteristics that the people who win possess. If you ever talk to anyone who has had tangible, material success, you will hear them retort the same story. What others see as an overnight success requires years and years of consistent work. From a celebrity to an athlete, from a millionaire to a serial entrepreneur, what you hear when they share their success are stories of when they were unsuccessful. You hear the dedication it took to get them where they are.

Successful people often acknowledge mentors, spouses, family members, and friends. Whenever they reveal secrets to success their motivation and inspiration are magnified. By listening to them, one can connect with things they've been through that make them human. People who are overcomers tell about their trials and tribulations because on the other side of that is victory! The only way to get to a place of victory is to go through trials and tribulations without stopping.

Some people have sustained head injuries. Some people have survived bad car accidents. Some people have a traumatic brain injury, or have had a stroke, and experienced emotional trauma, but they willed themselves to a better situation. They were determined to get healthy enough to make progress. Working in the medical field, I meet individuals who have a determination to succeed no matter what. They are so inspiring. They possess a positive attitude and, as a result, experience more positive outcomes. They will themselves to win with so much increased tenacity that their body then responds to their mental will to get better. I will reiterate this point because it's so important that it is worth reading twice. There is research to prove that a person can psychologically convince their mind to stay in such a positive state that their body then physiologically responds to their positive mindset.

I have witnessed people improve their health, regain their ability to talk, and walk. There is evidence of cancer patients being healed from their terminal disease because they did not accept anything else in their minds other than being healthy. They envisioned themselves getting better. They imagined themselves making improvements. They kept an attitude of gratitude. Yes, these were miracles and even when expecting a miracle, the atmosphere has to be set to receive it.

I am confident that you, too, can get to that place. It requires being so sure (mentally and spiritually) that you must constantly rebuke, refuse, cast down, and denounce anything contrary to what you believe. This is a daily duty that you must perform. You have to daily refuse, rebuke, denounce, and deny anything contrary to the positive things that you are working towards accomplishing. That takes incredible faith! It takes a consistent effort to hold onto a belief regardless of current circumstances.

Hold onto the promise that God gave you despite what else is happening around you or what other people say. Irrespective of how silly it may look to other people, hold onto the promise. This is personal. It's your dream! It's your vision! It's your purpose to fulfill! Embrace what God has put in you. You will persevere. You will win. You will overcome. You are a champion.

The Oxford dictionary defines a **champion** as someone who has defeated or surpassed all rivals and competition, especially in sports.

If you think of life as a competition, not that you're competing with anyone, but if you look at life as a battle or a fight, you know the battle is already won. You will come out as a winner. God has overcome the world! Repeat this statement, "I am more than a conqueror through Christ who loves me" (Romans 8:37).

The second definition of a **champion** is a person who fights or argues for a cause or on behalf of someone. When you use the word champion as a verb, it supports the cause of or defending. You are protecting your vision. You are not defensive, but you are defending a vision, a goal, a purpose, and a destiny.

An **overcomer** is a person who succeeds in dealing with or gaining control of some problem or difficulty.

No one is perfect. You're not always going to respond in the right way. You're not always going to be in control. What I like about the definition of an overcomer is it is a present participle, dealing with the present tense. Meaning it's a constant thing. As problems arise, an overcomer is constantly battling for victory. As an overcomer, you deal with situations in the present moment by continuously gaining control of some problem or difficulty. You are in the moment, gaining control, which means you must be able to analyze it while in it. So don't sleep. Stay woke.

If you notice you're losing control, return to the foundation. Go back to the basics. For me, that's prayer and declarations. It includes writing out my vision. If you have a vision board then you have written goals. You have the ability to finish it until the end. See yourself winning again. Drawing from the example that I provided about people who are sick who will themselves to better health, they are already seeing themselves healed. Keep that in mind as the definition of an overcomer.

Finally, **persevere**, which again is a verb, and means to continue. Here we go again. It is constant motion, doing something, continuing, moving on, and not being overtaken by a temporary situation. This is not permanent but continues to advance. Another definition is even in the face of difficulty, or with little or no prospect of success, a person continues. Wow! That is substantial! In other words, see with your spiritual eyes, and envision. Let me break that down.

Continue on the course of action. Execute the goals that you set for yourself on your vision board. Reflect on what you said that you would do. Connect to how you see yourself, and what you declared as your ultimate level of success. Do this **even in the face of difficulty or with little or no prospect of success; continue.** Even when you don't see success or when what you're doing doesn't have instant gratification, please continue to do it. Continue to be consistent. Knowing that, while you can't see it right now, all things are working together for your good. "All things work together for the good of those who love Him (God) and are called according to His purposes (Romans 8:28)." When you don't see the fruits of your labor right away, you must continue the work. "For I consider that the sufferings of this present time are not worth comparing with the glory that is to be revealed to us." (Romans 8:18).

MANIFESTATION THROUGH FOCUSED INTENTION

Don't let your vision change because of your temporary circumstances. Get back to the foundation. Get back to the fundamental principle of understanding that situations that are out of your control will occur. While you cannot control what is out of your control, you can manage your thoughts, emotions, statements, and responses. Monitor your reaction to things that are beyond your ability to manipulate. You have dominion through Christ Jesus to speak to those things that are not as they were (Romans 4:17). In other words, direct your thoughts towards a desired outcome, with the belief that through Christ, it will ultimately materialize in your reality.

FAITH

This entire chapter could be summarized in one word, and that is **faith**. Check your faith. Where is your belief? Are you wavering? Does your outcome change in your head based on the situation and the circumstances that you see? If so, that is not faith.

According to the Bible, **"faith** is the substance of things hoped for, and the evidence of things not seen." (Hebrews 11:1). Even when your environment seems contrary to everything you set out to accomplish, you must recalibrate. You must get back on track. Get back to the foundation of things you said you wanted to achieve. As things get more complex, increase your faith even more. Your faith must match the circumstances that you're going through. It must be enough to get you to a point where you can see past your immediate, temporary situation.

Faith it until you make it. You're too brilliant to not be a millionaire. Continue to affirm yourself. Meditate on what you want to see happen, not your current circumstances. It is time to see it again, and I don't mean one of the five senses: sight. I mean your vision.

> "Faith it until you make it."

Let's revisit what we've learned so far in this chapter. You were encouraged to conduct a genealogical search to find out what traits and characteristics run in your family through formal programs and by asking family members. Discovering and embracing your inner strength and purpose is a transformative journey that empowers you to unlock your true potential. By understanding and nurturing these aspects of yourself, you can live a life filled with passion, meaning, and fulfillment. Doing this will not only positively impact you but will position you to impact the world around you.

Remember, your journey toward embracing your inner strength and purpose is an ongoing process that requires self-reflection, self-belief, and commitment. Embrace this journey wholeheartedly and watch your life unfold with purpose and fulfillment.

REFLECTION

- What gifts and talents come naturally to you, which others may have to work for?

- Have you been aware of any areas where the enemy has tried to hinder your growth or steal your potential? How can you overcome these obstacles?

- How can you explore and uncover the skills and talents that are dominant in your family? How might this knowledge contribute to your understanding of your gifts?

- How do you define success? What are some common characteristics that successful people possess?

- Can you identify any mentors, family members, or friends who have played a significant role in your journey towards success?

- How have they motivated and supported you?

- How can a positive attitude and mindset contribute to your well-being and success? Can you implement any specific strategies or practices to maintain a positive mindset?

- How do you define yourself as a champion and an overcomer?

- How can you use visualization and positive affirmations to reinforce your belief in your vision?

Please document these questions and your responses to them.

CHAPTER FIVE

Your Roadmap (Past, Present, and Future)

Where are *you* going in your life? If you haven't thought about it, stop. Pause right here. Put a bookmark on this page and think about where you are going. At the beginning of each year, I make a list of goals. I always write things that I plan to accomplish. I realize that not all the goals I write are things I think will be completed by the end of the year. Indeed, if I never initiate or take the first step to complete it, it won't get done.

The Bible says to write the vision and make it plain. There is significance in writing things down. If nothing is written, ponder on what inspires you and what you aspire to do or be. Go ahead and jot down what pops into your head. Remember, it doesn't have to be pen and paper. It can be a note memo on your phone, iPad, laptop, sticky notes, or any other electronic device. Your thoughts can be informal. We will come back to this later in the book.

Are you the kind of person that doodles? Do you jot down notes on several pieces of scratch paper? Have you ever gone back to look at a paper and noticed several questions and different notes that only meant something to you? Maybe it was someone's name and phone number. Perhaps it was a thought or an idea. If you turned the paper sideways, there may have been something else unrelated to the rest of the information on the form. Or are you more organized? You may like to contain all your thoughts and ideas in a journal. If I could offer a suggestion, my suggestion would be the latter.

Have I said it enough throughout this book? Let me suggest it one more time: journal regularly. Initially, it doesn't have to be anything significant. It can be a thought that comes to you. It could be your experience for the day. It can be something that you want to say to someone but don't know how to start the conversation. It can be a thought about an invention, that you wonder why no one else has developed the idea. It is essential to write these things down because as quickly as a thought comes into your mind, it may leave.

The process usually goes something like this. You have a thought or a suggestion. You assume it hasn't been done because you've never paid attention to it before. The moment you write it down, you begin your research. Once you start investigating the topic, you are now committed to doing it. That is the power of writing things down. It is one action that leads to a series of consequential steps.

REVISITING THE PAST

Every so often, I go through my old things. The purpose is to clean and declutter. Most of the time, it makes room for more stuff. This one time, when I was decluttering, I ran across different ideas that I had written. As I filtered through my things, I noticed all the other ventures I had initiated over the years and the various people that I had encountered. I thought about all the employees that I had employed in my company. I wondered where they were, their walks of life, and their personal stories. All these different things helped to broaden my perspective. One clear thing was everyone had their own story. Likewise, it is good for you to know *your* story.

Do you need to go back through old shoeboxes and file cabinets to reflect on goals that you have accomplished? People often don't give themselves enough credit for everything they've accomplished because they constantly strive for more. It is so important to recognize a few things.

1. Take a look back from where you started.

2. Know where you're going. I encourage you to look even more profound than old paperwork and journals. In the last chapter, I discussed knowing where you come from and what is embedded in you. I encouraged the exploration of Ancestry.com, MyHeritage, and 23andMe.

MY LOVE FOR WATER

I have always loved the water. The water is so serene. My swimming is self-taught and needs to be more coordinated. If you saw me in the deep end of a pool, you would probably think that I was trying to keep myself from drowning. However, it didn't stop my love for water! After finishing graduate school, the decision to move back home to Chicago, in a high-rise apartment with a view of Lake Michigan, seemed like the only logical "lake-loving" thing to do. It was beautiful! Large windows with extended panes made for sitting and viewing the lake were a routine way to decompress following a long workday. After staring for so long, my worries disappeared into those waves. I would leave the window with renewed peace of mind.

PRESENT

Fast forward to today, water is still a place of serenity. I have a lovely pond in my backyard with a fountain. When the weather's nice, opening the sliding door to hear the water from the fountain cascade into the rest of the pond is a favorite pastime. The sound immediately allows my mind to escape to a happy place. The connection in all this culminated as I became aware of my ancestry results. I found out that my ancestors were from a tribe in Africa, right off the ocean coast. I researched to find that they have an ocean economy primarily based on fishing. As a result, much of their job markets are positions involving water. This was a fascinating discovery! Tropical islands put me in a state of euphoria! This may be true for you as well. However, the missing pieces all came together when that part of my ancestry was revealed.

Have you ever been drawn to something and you're not aware of its origin, but you're sure it must have a deeper meaning?

Bright colors and patterns draw me in the same way. As a child, I have always loved patterns, stripes, plaid, horizontal patterns and shapes, chevrons, and mixtures of rich patterns all woven into one. The brighter the color, the better!

GOD IDEAS

If you haven't discovered it by now, everything leads back to spiritual creation. Biology follows the Bible because it is the beginning of creation.

I believe in God. We were made in His image and His likeness. God made us imaginative creatures. Therefore, God gives you "God ideas!" As I have come to know God more, certain things come directly from Him. Sometimes, an idea wasn't even a thought in my mind until it was. In other words, I would not have known about this idea or thought about a business concept until it was imported into my brain. It was not my thought until it became a thought. Right? It may have come in the form of a dream. It may have come from looking at something on TV, but then my mind or imagination goes into a different realm.

Those outrageous ideas should be written down in those moments because they can become a reality. Those tend to be "God ideas!" At first, the picture may not be obvious, but as you explore more, you **"God ideas!"** can begin to assemble the pieces and develop a game plan (business plan). The way you approach it matters, especially if it's bigger than you. All the steps do not have to be perfect. It may require connecting to other people who can give you resources. Maybe it's an idea that you have little knowledge of. Be willing to research and invest in yourself.

I'll share with you something exciting that I recently watched. The host of a popular evening TV show was interviewed by the host of a syndicated radio show. The radio show host asked the TV show host,

"Did you ever dream that you would be in this situation? Did you ever dream that you would come to the United States? Did you ever dream that you would travel the world making people laugh and hosting a TV show?"

The TV show host responded, "No, this was not in my plan. This was not in my dream."

He advised people not to pursue their dreams because sometimes you can't dream outside of what you know. He explained if you've never been out of your immediate environment, then even your dreams may not be very big or very bold. I thought that was a phenomenal take on life! If I were to take a little bit of that message and add my spin, I would say, write your dreams down. If you don't dream about helping others, what you want to accomplish for yourself, and life goals at night, dream it on paper. When you think about concepts that are so big that they scared you, write them down and pray about them. Explore them, especially if they come up more than once because this could be a part of your purpose.

FUTURE

When it comes to having a purpose, which everyone on this earth has, know that if you don't complete that purpose, it will be achieved with or without you. You are a vehicle, a conduit. You are the individual in human form that God will use to complete the purpose. If, for whatever reason, you are unable to meet that purpose, the purpose moves on. If God tasked you with completing that purpose, ask God for the strength, wisdom, determination, and tenacity to do it and to complete the mission!

Let's discuss ways in which purpose manifests. If your purpose is to help people, that can appear in many ways. You can help people by working at the Small Business Association (SBA), being a teacher, working in the medical field, or being a beautician. It is also essential to consider that purpose can change over time. You may be operating in your purpose and not realize it.

Many people have job experiences that are a hodgepodge of skills. You may have worked in a lot of different career fields. Just because the fields were various doesn't mean that your purpose changed. Contrarily, there may be times when you have completed the purpose of that assignment. Then, it may be time to move to a different purpose.

After becoming a married woman, I noticed that my purpose changed. My purpose is different now than when I was a single woman. My purpose is even more distinct now than when I was a single mother. My purpose is different now than it was when I was a student. Your purpose can be elevated as different phases of life unfold.

REFLECTION

- At this phase, *where are you going?*

- Once you take the time to explore that, write it down.

- Within the contents of your responses you may be able to identify and then define your purpose.

- If you have written down many different things, reflect on your life journey and identify pivotal points.

- Write it out, almost like a road map. This will allow you to infer where your road will take you. Your experiences may seem like they are unrelated until you complete this exercise.

- You will be able to see a pattern, maybe a habit, and repeatedly identify the things you do. It can allow you to uncover what you do well. Although the jobs differed, you may find out that you provided leadership the entire time.

- On the contrary, you may be able to use another roadmap that helps you identify passive behaviors. Those self-deprecating and counterproductive habits must be acknowledged and snipped at the root.

Be vigilant about finding your purpose. Sometimes that's mentally, sometimes spiritually, sometimes it's encouraging yourself with scriptures and meditating on God's word until you get to a place where you believe you can live out your dreams, even if they're larger than you.

Here are some additional scriptures to help you.

"Let all things be done in decency and order" (1 Corinthians 14:40).

"God's word does not return void, but it shall do whatsoever He pleases and shall prosper in the things for which He sent it" (Isaiah 55:11).

"My grace is sufficient for thee: for my strength is made perfect in weakness" (2 Corinthians 12:9b). This means if you don't have the strength within your power to do it, God's strength is perfected in your weakness.

"He that has begun a good work in you will perform it until the day of Jesus Christ" (Philippians 1:6).

You can do all things through Christ who strengthens you! (Philippians 4:13).

Use tools to build yourself up spiritually. Don't quit. Keep trying. Believe that it is attainable. Create an outline for what you are going to do. Challenge yourself and try something new today. Maybe the idea hasn't changed that much but perhaps the way that you implement it needs to change.

Again, I ask the question, 'Where are you today?' Is there something unfinished you can accomplish better the second time? Use the wisdom and understanding that you've gained in life. Pray about it. Seek God's face and work towards it. In other words, change is inevitable. As time progresses, everything changes. Change occurs every nanosecond, every millisecond, every second, every minute, every hour of the day, every day of the week, every week of the month.

It's time to move forward. In preparation for your future, it's time for an inventory check on emotional baggage.

- As you look at your past experiences, can you revisit them now with more wisdom? Did you gain clarity?
- Can you speak about the last experience without hurt?
- What about the humiliation associated with a failure or a setback?
- Do you have a newfound perspective?
- Can you look at that thing for what it was?
- If you were to try it again, do you have more clarity? More wisdom?
- Can you implement strategies that you had not implemented before?
- Will time allow you to finish things you had not completed before?

This time, when you write down where you're going, it should include everything past, present, and where you see yourself going. You now have the navigation system you need to turn left, keep straight, turn right, or turn around. After reading chapters one, two, three, four, and now the information you've gained in this chapter, answer this question.

Where are you going?

CHAPTER SIX

Adopting Resolute Faith and Perseverance

The title of this book mentions the ability to overcome difficulties in life. We will spend some time defining the overcomer on a deeper level. The psychological and spiritual formation of overcoming will be explored. This chapter will conclude with steps on how to become an overcomer.

In chapter three, we discussed the innate traits you are born with that make you unique. God does not make mistakes. He created everything in His image and His likeness. God intentionally made you who you are and there are parts of you that reflect Him. The good things you gravitate towards may feel like second nature, but other people must learn to do them. These are things that God uniquely put inside of you. The practices that you don't like are bad habits that you've learned along the way. Just like you have learned those negative behaviors, you can unlearn them and replace them with positive attributes.

What makes you an overcomer? Let's look at the definition of an overcomer. According to Oxford, to **overcome** means to succeed in dealing with a problem or difficulty. To defeat an opponent. An opponent can be an obstacle; it doesn't always have to be a person. Another meaning of **overcomer** is to prevail, an emotion of overpowering or overwhelming.

As I was reading my Bible recently, a few words kept emerging. One was resolute. God always instructs us to be resolute amid adversity. If God has given you a dream and provided revelation, then resolute is a word you must know and thoroughly understand. Becoming so **resolute** or admirably purposeful, relentless, and unwavering is required to accomplish something that God shared with only you. It means to be adamant and unswerving.

To be **resolute** is unflinching. It is constant. It is committed. It is even stubborn. Think about stubborn people. If they want things a certain way, it is hard to sway or convince them otherwise. They cannot be easily persuaded to choose another option when they are committed.

What are some things that you have been committed to? Maybe you've been committed to losing weight. Maybe you were committed to a specific New Year's Eve resolution. Maybe you were committed to completing a degree or finishing school. Were you devoted to saving for an upcoming trip or to marriage? Now, think of all the sacrifices that you have made to keep that commitment. No matter how many challenges you have faced, you still return to that one thing. Wasn't it hard? Didn't the opposition make you regroup? Didn't the game plan change a little bit? But it did not keep you from meeting that end goal. That is the fabric of an overcomer. God defines an overcomer as being resolute.

I've experienced so many things in my life. All the "no's" that I've heard caused some people to say, "You've taken a lot of L's" or "Girl, you've had a lot of losses."

> **"When I can say that I learned something in the process, it is never a loss."**

They were not losses. They were experiences! They were challenges. If I'm still going, I don't consider it a loss. It was an experience in which I learned a lesson. Trust me, there are some things that I would never repeat. However, when I can say that I learned something in the process, it is never a loss.

People who are not in the same situation and don't have the same obligations as you may be able to criticize your timeline for accomplishing goals. Some goals took longer for me to complete, but I never gave up on them. I had to reprioritize and finish some goals before others, but I never stopped pursuing them. The plans that took longer to accomplish allowed me to learn, which was invaluable!

At the end of the experience, what other people saw as a loss, I said, "Wow, I would have never learned that had I not gone through the experience." I was grateful for the extra time; looking back, I wouldn't change anything about it. Some people say I would do it differently if I had to do it all over again. For me, I would do the same thing again, not because I did everything right. Not because I didn't experience pain, but the lesson that I learned wouldn't have been achieved if things were done differently. This is an example of when being an overcomer takes tenacity.

Tenacity, according to Oxford, is tending to keep a firm hold of something, clinging or adhering closely, and not readily relinquishing a position, principle, or course of action determined. Persisting in existence is not quickly dispelled.

Notice that none of these definitions include the word quick. Yet, some people feel that the goal won't be achieved if they haven't accomplished something within a specific time frame. I am going to introduce to you the very famous phrase that my pastor says to his congregation. "I rebuke your age!" Never think that you are too old to accomplish a dream. Society has a way of placing age stipulations on people. For example, it is internalized, and people feel it will never happen if they do not get married by the age of 25 or 30. Who said it would never happen if someone did not climb the corporate ladder to become an executive-level leader by age 40? Who said if a woman does not have a child by the age of 42, it will never happen? Society sets that standard, and people, in turn, place those unfortunate societal norms on themselves.

While placing these harsh timelines on us, no one thinks about what people will say after our personal goals have been met. Once you start your family, complete a degree, get married, or start a business, no one will dispute that. When you have the right people around you, they will revel in your achievements and celebrate your blessings with you no matter how long it takes. I would dare to say that you must get out of your head. Maybe you are your worst critic. Maybe you beat yourself up worse than a hater would. I say don't do it. You have a plan. Work on the plan.

Let me provide context. Let's say you want to achieve certain things within five years, so you set five-year goals. There are three goals in your five-year plan. By the end of your designated time, you've accomplished none of them, but you are working towards all three. Is that something to be upset about and decide to quit? Absolutely not! You are still making progress on all three of those goals, and that is wonderful!

I am a primary example of finishing my own goals later than anticipated. In my first year of college, I was enrolled in a school I initially did not want to attend. I never gave up on attending the university where I wanted to study. I went away to college for one year. Then returned home because my grades were poor.

I was not mature enough to handle that kind of freedom. Instead of going to my 8:00 AM lecture class, I stayed in bed. It was the best freedom, and I did exactly what I wanted. This included socializing and meeting new people, participating in extracurricular activities, attending games, and not prioritizing my class work. There were classes that I did very well in, but it wasn't enough to raise my cumulative GPA. I was an immature teenager living in the moment and not considering the long-term consequences of my actions. I was not applying myself. My parents didn't want me to waste any more college tuition when I was not focused on my coursework. I went back home and attended community college for one year and a semester.

After raising my GPA, I left community college in December and began at the university where I originally wanted to study. The story's moral is that I transferred to multiple schools as an undergraduate, eventually finishing my degree after five years and a summer.

After coming home and working for a year, I returned to earn my master's degree. Guess what? I also did not finish my master's degree in precisely two years. I worked while attending graduate school that first year. I took an extra semester and graduated in December instead of May. Let me tell you, once I got over the initial concern of racing against the clock, I became invested in learning the information. At that point, it became more critical for me to master the information than to rush to finish. As long my degree was "in progress" status, that was sufficient.

At first, I beat myself up about not graduating in May. The last semester of my graduate program happened so quickly that I finally stopped racing against my own time clock. At last, I was no longer immobilized by time. I knew when I graduated and started working in the field as a speech-language pathologist, no one was going to say, "Oh my gosh, it took her longer to graduate with her undergraduate degree. I can't believe she stayed an extra semester to finish her master's degree." No! No one said that. They said, "She is a speech-language pathologist." Again, I re-emphasize you are creating your own imaginary race by unnecessarily competing against the clock. You are creating anxiety because you are running against yourself and this unrealistic time clock that you have created in your mind.

Place your circumstances in this example. When you have a child (I don't care if it's through adoption methods, by marriage, biological, via surrogate, etc.,) people are going to say, "She's a mom," "He's a dad." However long it takes for you to become a wife, once you become a wife, people will say, "She's a wife." When you become a husband, no matter how long the process takes, people will call you a husband once the marriage has occurred. Whenever you become a business owner, no matter how many times you've tried different businesses and failed, people will identify you as a business owner. No text field on the articles of incorporation application asks an individual to indicate how many failed business ventures they've had. Don't unnecessarily pressure yourself to feel goals won't be achieved if you haven't accomplished your dreams by a certain age. That is a lie from the pits of hell. I rebuke that lie and encourage you to keep on overcoming!

You must have tough skin. You must be resolute. You must be tenacious. You must be dogmatic. It would be best if you operated in faith. Obscene faith! Unconventional faith! Crazy faith! Undeniable faith! Irrefutable faith! Remember, faith is the substance of things hoped for, the evidence of things not seen (Hebrews 11:1). If any of these areas still need improvement, return to the basics. Get to a place where you have spiritual balance. Whether that means praying more, meditating, exercising, detoxing, eating right, cleansing your body, fasting, praying, reading the Bible, journaling, and affirmations, find homeostasis.

I want to share a reference point from another life story. I used to run cross country. The most challenging time to continue running was when I first started. My legs would start to bother me as soon as I ran, maybe a quarter of a mile. They would get so heavy that I felt like walking, but I would not stop. I knew I had to get past the initial discomfort to continue going. My philosophy was that I don't care how slow I run; I refuse to walk. If I needed to run slower because I took off too fast, I would adjust my pace. I knew that it was not a sprint. It was a long-distance race. I knew if I could keep a good pace, I could sustain that pace for the entire race.

Soon enough, guess what happened? I would continue running, and the areas that initially bothered me would go numb. I wouldn't feel my legs anymore. I don't mean that in a concerning way. I mean that, in a sense, my body understood the assignment. My body made the necessary adjustments to finish the race. You must be very much like a distance runner. Towards the middle of the race, you may need to adjust your pace to not revert to walking.

The second thing I did as a distance runner was to have a "strategy" for the end of the race. As I got near the end, and maybe in that last half mile, I would increase the pace because I knew the end was close. I started to jog a little bit faster. I wouldn't speed faster than I knew I could sustain for the next half mile. It was gradual enough for me to maintain for another quarter of a mile and another tenth of a mile. Finally, in the last few hundred yards, I would sprint to the end and pass up about seven other runners. My coach was amazed!

I also ran track. So, I had the ability to sprint. That's why I used the word "strategy" for the end of the race. I want to focus for a moment on a multiplying factor. My coach yelled, screamed, and jumped up and down like I was his favorite sports team in a championship game. He could not believe I had the energy to sprint to the finish line. After witnessing that the first time, he was at every succeeding race, a few hundred yards from the finish line. What was his purpose? He was there saying, "Come on! Come on! Let's go! Pass her up!" Every single time, I would go from approximately 10th to second or third place because of all the runners I passed in the last few hundred yards.

This is the very same thing that you have within you. These are the very same characteristics that it takes to be an overcomer. This is the same mindset you must have and an unwillingness to give up. Having someone to cheer you on and support you along the way is of equal importance. My initial inclination to increase my pace at the end of the race yielded positive results. What kept me going was seeing and hearing my coach. I became dependent on his encouragement. When I was tired, his belief in me increased my faith in my capabilities to finish strong. If you have people questioning whether the time you have spent working towards accomplishing a goal is all worth it, replace them with people who will cheer you on and keep overcoming!

You will want to have a tribe who can encourage you, pray for you, enlighten you, and keep you accountable. The selection of the word tribe is intentional because you may not find all these things in one person. That one person can only edify and encourage you, and that is the most they can do. There will be another person who can pray for you; perhaps that's what they are assigned to do. Then, there will be another person who holds you accountable, and you trust them to do so without taking offense when they consistently check in on you. If you can have all that in one person without draining them (perhaps a spouse), that's wonderful. A spouse will be invested in you like no other individual. That one person could also be a godparent, parent, sibling, best friend, or mentor. Consider who those people are in your life. Often, they are already people who naturally show up in your life this way. You just haven't officially given them the title yet. Go ahead! Give them the title of tribe member!

STEPS ON HOW TO PERSEVERE

It is imperative to me that I don't simply tell you what to do but give specific instructions on how to get unstuck. Consider your spiritual balance because it has a substantial impact. Being spiritually unbalanced will overlap into every area of your life. Get back to the place where you are centered. You must intentionally shut out all noise and distractions to hear from God. Most distractions are thoughts that continue to swirl around in your head. A quiet space is where God will direct your path. The Bible says that God's word is a lamp unto our feet and a light unto our path (Psalm 119:105). Waiting on the Lord requires asking and then waiting to hear back before making the next move.

Isaiah 40:31 says, but those who wait on the Lord shall renew their strength. They shall mount up with wings like eagles. They shall run and not be weary, they shall walk and not faint. That's one scripture to remember as you wait on the Lord.

Another good Bible verse that encourages you to wait on the Lord is Psalms 27:14. "Wait on the Lord, be of good courage, and He shall strengthen your heart. Wait, I say on the Lord." If you are pressing into God's presence and want to know the next step because you feel like you have not received clarification from God, sometimes He wants you to be still for a season. It is necessary to listen to His instruction and receive His guidance.

I heard something interesting in passing that I want to pass on to you. Success takes people. God will always send **Success takes people.** someone with a message or a word of comfort, a word of enlightenment, or a word of confirmation. As mentioned in the story above, where my coach encouraged me to keep going, likewise is the role of having someone to help you maintain momentum. You can't do it all by yourself. God will send those people in your life. People enter your life for a reason, a season, or a lifetime. Confirm with God if that individual should be in your next chapter.

What if you wait, but you still don't receive an answer? Every so often, you may feel like you are far away from God. It may seem like you're asking about specific things and not getting a response, or you're trying different things, and nothing seems to go as planned.

1. Perhaps now is not the set time. Sit back and keep waiting on God.
2. Set aside time to pray.
3. Commit different scriptures to memory.
4. Set aside time to encourage yourself and state affirmations.
5. Set aside "me time."

For some people, that may be a walk in the park to decompress and get things off your mind. For others, that may be meditating, stretching, breathing, or exercising to relax. That may be yoga, hot yoga, or getting a massage to get all the tension out of your body. Whatever wellness practices you can incorporate regularly are necessary for moving forward. Self-care is a step that must be taken. It accompanies the mantra of caring for yourself mentally, physically, spiritually, and emotionally.

I want to share with you two thoughts. One is that I love to travel because I see how small things are whenever I hit a high altitude. Looking down at the clouds and seeing how beautiful things are from a bird's eye view helps me put everything into perspective. Seeing how small all the buildings, cars, and houses look makes me realize how we tend to magnify problems while in them. However, when we step back and get a bird's eye view, we see that our problems are temporary and minor.

Placing everything into perspective from the air

The second thing I want to share is that my friend group has always told me I do so well with self-care. I can recognize when I have had enough or need to do something for myself in order to return to a better mental space. Please know yourself well enough to know when to take a break. Learn how to implement self-care checks.

The most critical acknowledgment is when to seek professional help. There is nothing wrong with making an appointment to speak with someone skilled in helping you heal through trauma and significant loss. Not all problems can be resolved by picking yourself up by the bootstraps and reaching out to your core circle. Some people haven't healed enough to be vulnerable enough to share their problems with people close to them for fear of judgment. I pray that you have the courage to find the right professional who can give you the strategies needed to become a better version of yourself. Take it one step at a time.

The bottom line is when you are an overcomer, you do not give up. You must get a grip like a pit bull. You must clench onto something. Lock the promise in your jaw. It must be tight, so as life sends you a blow that knocks you off your feet, you still have that promise clenched in your teeth. Don't give up! Do not quit! I don't care if you slow down. If you don't stop, you are still winning!

REFLECTION

Conduct a wellness check on yourself.

- Where are you? Be honest about it.

- What do you need to get yourself to a better place? Sometimes, that would include getting something done, like a facial or body scrub, or some laser treatments for a refreshed look. For some people, that may be a little drastic, so it does not have to be that intrusive. For others, that may not be enough. Some people may need to take the step to seek professional help.

- The goal is to know when you have overextended yourself. Recognize it. Rectify it.

- Understand that you need a break before you get to the point of burnout.

- Determine if you would benefit from seeking a professional who can provide strategies to help you improve your mental health.

Start doing these self-care regimens to get in a better place mentally, emotionally, physically, and, of most importance, spiritually.

CHAPTER SEVEN

Avoid Crab Mentality: The Power of Collaboration

God will send people into your life for a season, a reason, or a lifetime. He will send people in your life to speak something into you that is so profound that it stops you in your tracks. You should give them your undivided attention because their words are accurate and thorough. When an individual you have recently met is capable of accurately understanding your entire life or is able to sum up what you are currently experiencing, it may be perceived as if they were divinely appointed. God must have sent them. This subsequent encounter was precisely that.

IT TAKES AN ARMY TO TAKE YOU DOWN

I met someone who I viewed as a mentor. More granularly, this person was sent into my life to help me birth something new. God ensured our paths would cross so she could help me create and complete an assigned purpose. She told me, "It takes an army to take you down. When people cannot support the light around you or the calling on your life, they know that they cannot take you down one-on-one. It's going to require numbers. It's going to require them to convince other people to believe what they say about you, so they can try to come against you and bring you down."

Her statement was mindboggling! I felt exposed. *How could she know what I've been through?* I thought. *She wasn't there.* As I recounted my life experiences, even from childhood, I felt that the theme of gathering multiple people and persuading them to go to war against me was accurate. It was so true that I felt it in the pit of my stomach. Flashes of memories came flooding into my consciousness. I was having an out-of-body experience as if those memories were scenes from a movie. Visions kept jumping around of every incident where this theme rang true.

From childhood to college to adulthood, it even spread across different settings of adulthood. From church to work to organizations, women who could not handle my light have always tried to convince other women to put my light out. When she said these words to me, I knew she was speaking the truth! I did not doubt that it was what God told her to say.

Take a moment to digest that story. Being a person that people attempt to shut down means they tell lies about you. They find negative things to say in an attempt to cover their insecurities. How do you respond when people say things about you that aren't true? How do you handle people who have done you wrong? What do you do? How do you maintain your character?

I learned early on that I had nothing to prove to anyone. I understand that not everyone will like me. My mom has always told me, 'You cannot please everyone. There will be some people who like you and others who don't like you, who you've perhaps done nothing to. There's nothing that you can do about that. All you can do is be yourself.' That advice has stayed with me throughout my entire life. When it comes to self-worth and self-value, I have a very healthy dose of that. I can credit my mom for instilling in me a lifetime of confidence.

Up to this point, we've explored winning characteristics. We've learned about establishing goals. We've defined what it means to be an overcomer. Knowing where you come from and where you are going was reviewed. We've emphasized how your innate ability to win can sustain you through life's difficulties. Can I share something with you? If you feel that you have to prove every person wrong who has said something negative about you or plotted against you, you are already losing. When people come against you with unfounded lies and rumors, chasing them down depletes your energy. It is distracting and takes you away from the very purpose that you are working towards achieving. Continuing in this way can get you so far from your purpose that you focus less on what you were put here to do and more on proving to people that you are the opposite of whatever attributes they have used to define you.

> **"If you feel that you have to prove every person wrong who has said something negative about you or plotted against you, you are already losing."**

God will fight your battles. God will prepare a table for you in the presence of your enemies. When you stay loyal to God and His purpose, God will be glorified. When you yield to God to be His vessel, there are things He can do with your life that no man can take from you or take credit for giving to you.

HEAVY IS THE HEAD THAT WEARS THE CROWN

I want to talk to my queens for a moment. Queens possess a confident presence. Most have strength and self-assurance because they know exactly who they are. I, too, wear a crown. It may tilt to the left or the right. I may go through experiences that almost cause my crown to fall. There have been times when my crown flipped in the air, and I have had to catch it in mid-air and put it back on my head. However, I am reminded never to let anyone define me. My actions, character, personality, and integrity exemplify who I am.

There may be moments when you lose your cool. Maybe you fly off the handle. Perhaps you don't respond to things in a calm manner or the way that you would like to respond. RESET! Gather your crown and put it back in its rightful place on your head. If you begin to question yourself at any moment and ask, 'Am I really who they say I am?' You've allowed their tainted image of you to be ingrained into your mind. You've permitted that toxicity in your system. The Bible says, resist the enemy, and he will flee. You cannot give in to anyone whose only assignment is to knock you down. It is called jealousy, which, most of the time, is rooted in envy.

Seek to find the reason why people do the things they do. What is their hidden agenda? In many cases, you are in a place where they wish they were. A person's insults often reveal their insecurities. If you remove the insult from the statement, you will often see that person's insecurities screaming so loudly. At that moment, you realize their words have less to do with you or what you did and more to do with how they feel about themselves. Often, people will project their insecurities onto you. It is your job to analyze the source and reject it. Return to sender. This is not a request to get into a verbal spat. Simply reject it and do not let it settle in your spirit or fester in your mind.

From a spiritual perspective, understand that the enemy seeks to destroy the light that you carry. Why? Because darkness and light cannot dwell in the same place. Your light causes those who are dark or in darkness to be exposed. There are several reasons why people find themselves in dark places. Your goal is not to dim your light to make others feel comfortable. I learned a song in Vacation Bible School called "This Little Light of Mine." The words are, "This little light of mine, I'm going to let it shine…hide it under a bushel, no! I'm going to let it shine."

Using a song that sounds like a nursery rhyme is a bit much. I get it. I understand your concern about using song lyrics and catchy rhythms to solve real-world problems. It may seem primitive at first glance. However, at times, the most effective way to disentangle life's biggest entrapments is to simplify. Finding the lessons packaged in song lyrics can be incredibly powerful and impactful.

Words are powerful!

When your intentions are pure, and your goal is to genuinely help people, know there will always be opposition. The naysayers and their noise should never be louder than the noise in your mind telling you to stay focused and keep going. Rather than hide your magnificence, use it to put a demand on those who are underperforming. Elevate your morale so that people around you are inclined to operate at a higher standard.

YOU ARE A WINNER!

You will get through this! Your purpose is more significant than the people in front of you, the naysayers, and the boos because right across from them are the cheers and yells from people who are rooting for you and the people who believe in your vision. There will be individuals who are fearless in supporting your vision. Some people see your drive, and instead of being intimidated by it, they celebrate it.

Realize that people who mean you malice and harm and who are deceitful are usually those who don't know you. They become intimidated when they see you operate in your element. In the Black community especially, we have a problem celebrating others. When others are doing well, we tend to see them as competition instead of cheering them on. I was fortunate to have generations of powerful women who celebrated other women. My grandmothers (both maternal and paternal) were women who celebrated other women. They were not jealous-spirited women. They were not spiteful or envious. My mother and my aunts are women who celebrate women. They encourage, illuminate, and speak positive things about other women. They befriend those kinds of people because they recognize them as individuals to have in their circle.

INVENTORY ASSESSMENT

Could you do a deep dive? Take inventory and determine if you are the type of individual who gets intimidated by people who are doing well. Do you find a reason to dislike someone that you barely know? Are you the person who cheers for others doing well, even if you don't know them? You may be watching their journey from afar. Do you admire their journey? Do you celebrate them? Do you encourage them? Have you ever told someone, 'I don't know you, but you are working, and I see the work that you're doing?' Have you ever revealed to someone that they have a certain aura, and when they enter a room, they light it up? Have you ever disclosed to someone that they are the kind of person you want to be around?

I challenge you to take inventory to determine if you are a celebrator or a hater. Figure out if you are a detractor or a promoter. Once you identify that, find out the origin of those emotions. The last thing that you want to do, mainly because it's so disheartening as an adult, is carry around trauma or hurt that happened from your childhood. Those emotions should not hold you hostage or keep you in captivity. It contradicts who you are called to be. It's not fair to the crown that is waiting to be worn. It is unacceptable to the people waiting for you to walk into your purpose so that you can help them reach their destiny.

> "It's so disheartening as an adult, to carry around trauma or hurt that happened from your childhood."

Once you've identified where those emotions come from, if you are a detractor, release those things. Declare today that you will no longer allow them to keep you hostage, to hold you back, to pull you down. Jealousy, envy, and baggage will weigh you down so much that you end up being worn out, in a bad mood, and constantly searching for the next person to assault verbally. It's so distracting that it keeps you from being who you are called to be. You are called to walk in your authority. You are called to be inspirational. You are called to be someone other people look up to and admire.

On the other hand, if you have identified that you are a promoter, celebrate other people doing good things, attract light, and like to be surrounded by like-minded people; then I challenge you to see who you can mentor. That person may be the same age as you but needs your mentorship to take them to their next career level. It may be someone younger than you, a daughter or son. It could be a godchild. It may be a neighbor. You may be a teacher or have a student you know needs guidance.

TIME TO BUILD

If you've already determined that you are a promoter, I also challenge you to build a circle of women who are celebrators. Build a circle of influencers, game changers, and other phenomenal individuals. Imagine the change you can make bringing together these wonderfully dynamic people who seek to uplift, not compete, to challenge, not tear down, and to build, not destroy each other. Think of the lives that will be changed by working together. Women keep this earth moving. Women set the standard. Women are nurturers. Women have the emotional capacity to lead the world.

> "Build a circle of women who are celebrators. Build a circle of influencers, game changers, and other phenomenal individuals."

My challenge to you in this chapter is to build your army. Instead of an army to conquer people, let it be an army that uplifts. Let's break the curse on the Black community, where women have been taught to compete against each other. Let's obliterate the crabs in a barrel mentality. Rather than doing that, let's build an army of women who can teach younger generations. Whether it's being a mother, a nurturer, a caregiver, creating several revenue streams, investing, serial entrepreneurship, becoming a franchise owner, building schools, building safe places for mental health, or health and wellness...whatever it is, you have something to give. Now, queen, please pick up your crown and put it on. Do not let anyone or any circumstance cause it to fall.

REFLECTION

The takeaway from the readings of this chapter is to know yourself fundamentally. Know who you are as a person. Know the intentions of your heart. Whatever your gift, identify the areas in which you excel. Identify your areas of strength.

Are you a detractor or promoter?

Get rid of those detracting behaviors.

Replace them with promoting behaviors.

CHAPTER EIGHT

Harnessing Confidence Through Affirmations, Emotional Intelligence, And New Beginnings

There comes a time in everyone's life when cycles complete. Seasons come to an end. The year concludes in 12 months. Various goals must come to fruition and materialize. There is an appointed time for everything. In the Bible, the number eight means new beginnings. The significance of this chapter is that the number of new beginnings implies that it is time to finish incomplete projects so that you can access your fresh start. When many plans are happening simultaneously, and it feels like there are a lot of moving pieces, but nothing has entirely fallen into place, fret not. Stay on the path of completion.

Sometimes, we expect a grand finale to signal the end of something, but that's not always the case. Culminations can happen quietly, without much activity. Often, we may not even realize that something has concluded because our perception of its importance has shifted. Before we know it, we've already started something new.

As we reflect on our journey, seeking guidance and inspiration from God can be helpful. We can find solace and clarity by acknowledging and inviting His presence. Writing down our goals, to-do lists, or checklists and actively working towards achieving them can also help us to recognize and appreciate our progress. It allows us to view how many items we have completed and reminds us of what we have accomplished.

Beginning something new takes confidence. **Confidence** is the feeling or belief that one can rely on someone or something. Confidence is firm trust. A confident person feels sure about the truth of something. There are certain things that you know about yourself that you can say with 100% confidence that you do. It is a character trait. It is a personality type. It is a characteristic, behavior, or value of your identity. Moreover, you can identify things with 100% confidence that you are not. You are not a liar, untrustworthy, or unfaithful.

How do you embed confidence into the fiber of who you are? This conversation is

> **"Self-talk is highly essential."**

about what you say daily in the mirror that no one else knows. Self-talk is highly essential. Maybe you don't say it aloud, but you encourage yourself in your head. The pep talk you give yourself to maintain confidence before you go in front of a crowd and operate in your greatness is self-talk!

Have you ever encountered someone who confidently spoke about various topics, even though you knew their knowledge and expertise were limited compared to yours? Interestingly, their confidence could make others believe they were highly knowledgeable. They may possess a natural charisma or the ability to speak convincingly. It's also possible that they worked on building their confidence privately before showcasing it to the world.

Focus on enhancing your expertise and knowledge in multiple areas. While confidence and charisma can make a person appear knowledgeable, backing it up with actual expertise is vital. Continuously learning and gaining expertise will boost your confidence and ensure you can effectively communicate and contribute to various discussions and situations. Invest time expanding your knowledge and honing your skills to become well-rounded and confident.

People can see through false confidence. A confident person is not self-inflated. The unhealthy type of self-confidence when someone tries to project an exaggeratedly confident, larger-than-life persona to overcompensate for insecurities is not the aura to emulate. Reject the self-confidence that is inflated that people can identify as an act. It not only lacks integrity, but it is also detrimental.

There are certain situations when faking it until you make it can be positive. For instance, if you are interviewing for a position and feel nervous about your abilities. Projecting confidence and acting as if you are capable can boost self-belief. This can lead to competence and success if a dedicated effort is continuously put towards improvement. You've gotten the job; now, you must prove that you will put forth the effort to stay in that position. Give yourself opportunities to improve your confidence over a period of time. The more chances you have to practice being confident in various situations, the better you will be at embedding it into how you present yourself.

AFFIRMATIONS

Affirmations are a great way to build confidence. For example, you get up daily, look in the mirror, and say, "I am not afraid to pursue my dreams.

I am not afraid of the consequences that may occur from stepping out to establish myself in the area of (fill in the blank). I am not afraid to do what I love. I will be successful in this area." At times, your confidence may waver, but it does not change your authenticity. There may be situations when you feel rejected, temporarily impacting your confidence. There may be times when you don't feel supported, and that may temporarily cause self-doubt.

Confidence is embedded in a feeling of self-assurance, which derives from one's appreciation of one's abilities or qualities. An example of this may be someone telling you that your hair is naturally brown, and you know for a fact that your hair is naturally blonde. You are self-assured that they are mistaken, which is the same attitude that confidence portrays.

When you are assured, even if it's just to fake it until you make it, keep behaving that way until you believe it. Affirm yourself often. For those individuals who lack confidence, this may be an exercise for you to practice daily. Overall, you may be a confident person, but one area may challenge your self-confidence. Again, reassuring yourself that you can accomplish whatever that area demands means incorporating daily doses of faith.

THE 21-90 RULE

When you constantly reassure yourself, it leaves little room for doubt to sneak in and for you to second-guess your abilities. Instead, operate and remain in a state of certainty. Please continue to do this repeatedly until it becomes a habit, I believe that everyone has heard the rule that it takes 21 days to form a habit (I'm going to give you the second part of that) and 90 days to make it a permanent lifestyle change. A 21-90 rule states that it takes 21 days to make a habit and 90 days to make it a permanent lifestyle change. So let me ask you a series of thought provoking questions.

What would happen if you fed yourself positive things? What would happen if you regularly spoke aloud self-reassuring thoughts?

Where could you be in 90 days? Just the mere thought of that should make you smile. Your wheels should be turning in the areas that need improvement.

Remember, you must be able to visualize yourself past the point where your immediate circumstances have placed you.

Let me take a moment to explain the kind of assertiveness to exude. Confidence is the behavior of someone triumphant. Recall the traits of an overcomer. Let's avoid succumbing to our previous tragedies, mistakes, and failures. You want to, in some cases, overdose on confidence until you can maintain a healthy level. You must train your mind to know the difference between temporary and permanent so your emotions can align accordingly.

Your mind must be trained not to assign permanent emotions to a temporary situation. I will write that again so you can read it twice because it's essential. Train

> **"Train your mind so that you do not assign permanent emotions to a temporary situation."**

your mind so that you do not assign permanent emotions to a temporary situation. Practice confidence until your mind understands isolated situations and doesn't treat trials and tribulations as the total of who you are. You are not a wounded soul. You are a warrior! You are not a victim. You are a victor!

HOW TO CREATE AFFIRMATIONS

Affirmations are powerful! They have done wonders in my life. I created affirmations for my husband when I was single because they were based on the characteristics that I wanted in a husband. Once I got married, my affirmations changed and became more specific based on his role as the husband, father, and head of the household. I created affirmations for my family and how I wanted to be treated as the mother and wife in the household. I created affirmations to speak over my children. I want to teach you how to create affirmations for different areas in your life so that you can experience change as you embark on new beginnings.

For example, I want to use a general affirmation for someone who provides a service. When creating affirmations for success, it may read as follows- I will help others. Others will come to me for assistance because of my quality of work. The additional detail I take to ensure that others are happy with my work keeps me in high demand. The extra love and compassion I put into servicing those needing help will have others talking about my business. People familiar with my work ethic will champion me and bring customers to me. Other people will support me and be word-of-mouth marketers who bring customers to me. As a result, the compassion, care, and attention that I put into differentiating my services from other businesses will allow me to reap financial benefits.

If you want to place a specific number on that financial report, you have every right to do so. The focus is on something other than making money. If you want to quantify success, who am I to tell you that you cannot?

However, if your business is coupled with a purpose and passion, walking in your purpose will provide a sense of fulfillment. Be happy to share your gift with others as a business owner, and the business will never just be about making money. Contrarily, if you are not making money as a business owner, you are volunteering your services. With 1,000% confidence, when you provide a good service, you are worth every penny and, therefore, need to know your worth and charge accordingly.

AFFIRMATIONS USING BIBLE SCRIPTURES

For a blessing to come from God, there's often something that God requires of you. The blessings of God are attached to obedience. Deuteronomy 28:1-14 contains verses relating to blessings for obedience. These verses are incredible to say aloud because they are the promises of God. You can put 'I' in the verse to make it personal. 'Lord, you promise if I fully obey your word and keep all your commandments, that you will set me high above all nations of the world. I thank you, Lord, that my towns and my fields are blessed. My children and my crops are blessed. I thank you that my offspring, my herds, and flocks are blessed. My fruit baskets and breadboards are blessed. Wherever I go and whatever I do, I am blessed.'

'Lord, you will conquer my enemies when they attack. They will attack from one direction, but they will scatter from me in seven. Lord, you guarantee a blessing in everything I do. You will fill my storehouses with grain. Lord, you will bless me and the land that you gave me. If I obey the commands of you, Lord, my God, and walk in your ways, you will establish me as your holy people. You swore this you would do. All nations of the world will see that I am yours, and I am claimed by you, Lord, and they will stand in awe of you.'

'Lord, you will give prosperity and the land that you swore to my ancestors to give me. Blessing me with many children, numerous livestock, and abundant crops. You will send rain at the proper time, and I thank you for the rain. God, I thank you that it comes from your rich treasures in Heaven. You will bless all the work that I do because you have caused me to lend to many nations, and I will never need to borrow. God, you said if I listen to the commandments that you have given and if I carefully obey them, you will make me the head and not the tail. Therefore, I am the head and not the tail. I am always above and never beneath.' Don't be afraid to seek out the Bible in whatever area that you want to create an affirmation, and use scripture as your daily declarations.

In what areas would you like to see God move? For example, if you give good advice naturally and want to give more in-depth advice, you may wish to get formal training. Wherever the direction God is leading you, get training in that area to help you gain discipline with your gift.

Your affirmation could be, 'I am being shaped into a counselor. I am being shaped to counsel people. I am taking courses to complete a certification that will allow me to use my gift to guide people. I find great joy in helping people solve problems. I find great joy in providing wisdom in areas where people don't know how to solve problems.

'My gift of counseling is becoming sharper and sharper each day. My gift of counseling is being fine-tuned. People will seek me for counsel. I will complete the coursework for the academic achievements needed to earn my counseling degree/certificate. I will complete my bachelor's degree. I will complete my master's degree.'

'My professors are already in place for me. My professors will be supportive. My professors will pour into me. My professors will guide me in this field of (fill in the blank) and will become my mentors. My program will be easy for me. I will gain knowledge in (fill in the blank), and opportunities will never cease to present themselves. God will use me to create a new venue in the realm of (fill in the blank).'

Please use the above examples as a template. Replace your desires with the samples that I have provided. Include whatever you want to see manifest in your life in your affirmations. Contrarily, if there are areas where you need to improve. Create affirmations to strengthen your problematic areas. If you know that you have an issue with trusting people and it hinders your ability to establish relationships with new people, create an affirmation that includes increasing trust.

For example, 'I am trustworthy, and I trust others. My trust increases daily, and my discernment allows me to know who to trust and who not to trust. Because I trust God, He will not lead me astray.'

'I am establishing relationships with trustworthy people every day. These relationships allow me to partner with trustworthy individuals who can help me pursue my business endeavors. I only engage in business with trustworthy people. Trustworthy people find me. I am trustworthy, so I attract trustworthy people.'

There are always scriptures that can be added to affirmations. A scripture that comes to mind is, 'Trust in the Lord with all thy heart and lean not to thy understanding, but in all thy ways acknowledge Him, and He shall direct thy path' (Proverbs 3:5-6). Adding a scripture to that affirmation can look like this: I am trustworthy and deal with trustworthy people because I trust in you, God. Your words say to trust in the Lord and lean not to my understanding.

'Your word says seek ye first the kingdom of God, and His righteousness, and all these things will be added unto me. I trust you because I am leaning not toward my understanding, but I'm acknowledging you and allowing you to direct my path. I know that you will only bring trustworthy people on my path.'

Analyze what it is that you want to change. Hear from the Lord so that He can provide guidance. It requires spending time reading His word. God will give you the words to speak as you hear from Him. Write those things down and speak them daily. Say what you want to see until you begin to see what you say. Your words have power.

Affirmation is just one part. The other part is creating an atmosphere of praise. Praise gets you ready to receive what you are expecting. It is okay to expect things from God. It is okay to expect good things to come into your life. Trouble happens. Trials and tribulations occur. Nobody must ask for those things to happen; they show up.

There is nothing wrong with putting a demand on God to have good things happen to you and for you to fully expect that good things will occur. When you praise God, you set the expectation that God will honor His word. Constant praise puts you in a place of gratitude. Look at everything you have, and don't focus on what you lack. When creating an atmosphere of praise, focusing on what you lack is counterproductive. It does the opposite of setting the atmosphere. The goal is to create an atmosphere that invites God into your life.

Notice the subtleties in nature. They are signs of God's presence. Lately, I have been noticing birds. They are everywhere I go. They seem to chirp so loudly that I must stop whatever I'm doing and take notice. "Chirp, chirp, chirp, chirp" is all I hear. I remember the Bible verse, 'Let everything that have breath praise the Lord' (Psalms 150:6).

I have seen baby birds in my driveway. I've seen birds at the drive-through when I'm trying to order food. The birds chirped so loudly, near the speaker, that I had to talk over them so that the lady in the restaurant could hear my order. Birds have been coming very close to me when I am walking. Normally, birds will fly away when you walk near them. Instead, I was the one going in the opposite direction.

Acknowledging that these were signs of God's presence, I asked God, 'What are you trying to show me with these birds?' I was reminded of a scripture that even the birds praise God. My sister brought to my attention that they were probably praising God. God created every living creature, male and female He created them. He made the animals in the sea, the farm animals, the animals on land, and the fowl of the air. All animals worship God.

When you are at a place where you want to see things manifest in your life, you must create an atmosphere of praise. State your affirmations and seek God. Ask God to show you what to write. As He reveals them to you, write them down. Understand that writing doesn't have to be pen & paper. Affirmations can be created using your smartphone. You can set a reminder on your smartphone calendar and text your affirmations in the notes section of your appointment on the calendar. Set it to recur daily, and now you are reminded of those affirmations to read. Another idea is to set a reminder on your Google Home or Alexa so you don't forget to say your affirmations daily.

Remember, the tool for manifestation is praise so that you set the atmosphere to say your affirmations. The purpose of our affirmations is to speak it until you see it. Shift how you feel. Believe that things can change, and change will manifest in your life.

EMOTIONAL INTELLIGENCE

Emotional intelligence (EI) can be a foundation for confidence by helping you navigate social interactions, build strong relationships, and effectively communicate thoughts and feelings. EI, otherwise known as emotional quotient (EQ) is the ability to recognize, practice, and master your emotions in meaningful ways to relieve stress, connect with others, empathize, overcome challenges, and lessen disputes.[2]

EI has four domains: self-awareness, self-management, social awareness, and relationship management. As situations occur, you have the responsibility to manage your emotions. Different challenges will require other emotions. The goal is to maintain your emotional state when different circumstances present themselves.

Life can be ruthless! In an ideal situation, you would only have to encounter people who love and respect you. In a perfect world, you would be well respected in society, and mere association with you would give

---

[2] Segal, Jeanne, Smith, Melinda, Robinson, Lawrence, and Shubin, Jennifer, October 2019, retrieved from: https://www.helpguide.org/articles/mental-health/emotional-intelligence-eq.htm

others an advantage. All your colleagues would be people who respect and support you, BUT that is not the real world.

How do you deal with people who are challenging to get along with?

How do you deal with people who have low morale?

How do you deal with people who take their anger out on you or are overly anxious?

Someone with a high EQ is not impulsive or hasty in their reactions. These individuals take the time to think about their response before they blurt it out.

People who have high EQ are typically good judges of character. They can identify weaknesses and strengths in themselves. You must be able to do the same. When you identify your triggers, you can learn how to avoid being triggered.

Have you ever been so triggered that you surprised yourself with your reaction?

Have you ever had a situation that made you so angry, and you became furious so quickly that it scared you?

Understanding your triggers, strengths, and weaknesses will allow you to prepare a well-thought-out response so that the same things don't repeatedly provoke you.

You can learn a healthy way to respond to unexpected and unfavorable circumstances.

Someone who operates with high EQ can let go of mistakes. They don't hold grudges. They are not easily offended and know how to deal with toxic people. This one is very important because, again, in an ideal world, you won't have toxic people around you. That falsity is wishful thinking but isn't reality. You will have to deal with toxic people, albeit in social circles, professional gatherings, or religious settings. Family gatherings can also be a setting for unhealthy and unchecked behaviors. Some of your family members may be the most toxic people you know. This falls into the relationship management category of EI.

Someone who has high EQ can neutralize a toxic person, and for some people, that means walking away and letting them argue with themselves. For others, that means not taking it personally because it's not your problem; it's their problem. Still, for others, it's providing a listening ear but not internalizing things or setting boundaries. When you walk away from that person, you leave the problems they have just dumped on you. You walk away from the negative statements that they carelessly vomit out of their mouth. Moreover, neutralizing someone else's emotional baggage is operating in emotional regulation. When you can reduce how intense an emotion feels, you can regulate your emotions so that you don't respond to certain situations the way you used to.

There's a great test available on EI. As a leader or if you own a business, the assessment will be an excellent opportunity to learn your boundary lines in each of the four areas EQ assesses. If you have never taken an EI test, I recommend that you do. The Emotional Quotient Inventory (EQ-i) 2.0 is a psychometric, validated assessment instrument. The questions help one to self-assess the areas that comprise EI.

(https://www.eitrainingcompany.com/eq-i/).

The composite areas are Self-Perception, Self-Expression, Interpersonal, Decision Making, and Stress Management. It is one of the most respected and recognized EI assessment instruments worldwide and details a robust and intuitive framework to address questions related to leadership. Here is the website to learn more- https://www.eitrainingcompany.com/eq-i/. I encourage you to use it to identify your strengths and weaknesses within the EI domains.

Let me share a quick story about self-awareness and self-management. Public speaking comes easily for some people, but for others, it is extremely difficult to the point where they experience so much fear and anxiety that they cannot bring themselves to speak in front of a crowd. EI, on a very bare-bones level, is understanding the origin of the anxiety and fear of public speaking. This is **self-awareness**. The **self-management** portion of EI would be the ability to switch gears and switch emotions from anxiety to calmness. Feelings of anxiety come from being excessively overwhelmed. When a person is constantly moving (whether physically or in their mind), that movement, movement, movement, and constant feelings of go, go, go create more fear. Switching emotions from being anxious to being calm requires having less activity. Those feelings of go, go, go need to be counteracted with slow, slow, slow. Slow things down. Slow down your mind. Slow down your thoughts.

Other people may be quick-tempered. Becoming easily triggered may be a character flaw. An individual may learn to lighten the mood by learning to laugh at situations or tell a joke. It allows one's emotions to switch from anger to amusement or humor. This is an example of **self-management**. EI also allows one to understand the consequences and repercussions of responding angrily and the impact it can have on everything the individual worked hard to accomplish. The individual may then resolve to react more rationally. That is the ability to regulate emotions. While this is **self-management**, it is also **social awareness**.

Conversely, someone who lacks EI is often insensitive or rude. They are inconsiderate, so they may blurt out harmful things. They don't take the time to think about what their words will mean to someone else or the reaction that someone else may have to them. This is an example of someone who lacks **self-awareness**. They lack **social awareness** that their words are insensitive and inappropriate for that setting. Not considering the ramifications of their actions can also overlap with relationship management.

Individuals can be selfish when they lack EI because everything revolves around them. Responses may often be tactless. They say things without giving any thought to their words. They operate without a filter. They say the first thing that comes to their mind and lack the maturity to think before speaking.

No one is perfect. Sometimes, people will say things that are not meant to be harmful to others, but each person's experience is different, so they may react to the words being spoken because it triggers them. However, someone regulating their emotions may say something without thinking, and once it's out there, they may retract it or apologize when they see it has offended someone.

I encourage you to take the test to understand where you are within these different domains of EI. The reference I provided further details the categories and subcategories of the assessment. When you understand your own EI, it helps you empathize more with others. I challenge you in this chapter to follow the resources, take the test, and identify your strengths and weaknesses. Once that is determined, go further to set goals that are Specific, Measurable, Achievable, Relevant, and Time-based (SMART) for some areas where weaknesses have been identified. A SMART goal is an acronym for those who need to become more familiar with setting goals, leading us to the next chapter.[3]

---

[3] {Meyer, Paul J. (2003) Attitude is Everything: If You Want to Succeed Above and Beyond, retrieved from https://www.projectsmart.co.uk/smart-goals/brief-history-of-smart-goals.php

REFLECTION

We've explored the ins and outs of self-discovery and personal growth.

It has become crystal clear that self-discovery isn't something you check off a to-do list and call it a day. It's a lifelong process. It's about continuously digging deeper, exploring new aspects of ourselves, and embracing the changes that come our way.

Self-reflection and confidence are necessary tools to begin anew. It's all about recognizing strengths and unique abilities without comparing yourself to others. Let's be honest; we're all on our paths, which makes it so beautiful.

EI is a gem that is a gateway to confidence. It helps navigate emotions and improve communication and how we connect to others. By sharpening our EI, we can build better relationships and gracefully handle life's curveballs.

Keep exploring. Keep learning, growing, and evolving. Believe in yourself and the incredible power that lies within you. Your journey is just commencing, and I can't wait to see where it takes you. Embrace the challenges, embrace the beauty of self-discovery, and know that you have everything it takes to create a truly fulfilling life. I hope that this chapter has provided valuable guidance for your continued advancement.

CHAPTER NINE

The Framework of Goal Setting and Small Victories

There comes a point in every overcomer's life when you must set goals. I am inclined to say it is impossible to be an overcomer without setting goals. Goal setting is an easy task. It's the **execution** of goals that requires consistent work. In this chapter, I will highlight the necessary steps to set goals.

The first step in setting goals is to make them obtainable. I mentioned SMART goals at the close of the last chapter. When you create goals, you want them to be specific. An elusive goal lacks guidance and will cause one to lose track multiple times because the goal lacks clarity. Let's use the example of being a millionaire by the end of this year. Okay...well... that's a goal...but is it specific? No. It's not detailed enough. Oftentimes, when a goal is set, mini-goals should ensue. Setting a goal at the beginning of the year for something you want to accomplish by the end of the year without putting any steps in between is vague.

Time goes by so quickly that getting off track throughout the year is easy. Along with setting goals, another word for mini goals is objectives. Objectives would be the targets that must be met to accomplish the goal.

A vague goal, like I want to be a millionaire by the end of this year, can be made more **specific** by creating objectives that specify how the plan will be met.

The M, as you recall, in SMART goal is **measurable**. I want to be a millionaire by the end of this year. Is that measurable? Yes. Sure, it is. The end of the year is December 31st at 11:59 pm. I have yet to meet the goal if I had not earned or made a million dollars by then. It is measurable.

Achievable is the A in SMART. Is earning a million dollars by the end of this year achievable? Sure, it is. If it doesn't get accomplished, will it ruin one's ego? Will it destroy your self-confidence? Will it be so discouraging that it prevents making more goals because that goal wasn't accomplished? That's something that one must ask oneself. When creating an achievable goal, be realistic about whether the goal can be achieved within the time frame allotted. The creator of the goal determines the time frame. If it's not enough time, allocate more time to complete the goal.

The R in SMART is **relevant**. The goal has to be rewarding enough to work towards achieving. When setting a goal, if it lacks interest, the goal will lose its gusto by day two, and it will be replaced by something more interesting. Let's take, for instance, losing weight. If a person wants to lose weight in a month because their birthday is at the end of the month, planning a birthday party would involve several steps. One would need to coordinate an outfit, a hairstyle, and what accessories will be selected to set off the new look. Finding a location, calling venues, and sending out invitations are all a part of preparing for the seamless implementation of the event. An itinerary of the birthday weekend may include a pamper session the day before and more celebrations to follow.

Again, if this individual's birthday is at the end of the month, planning would have been done before a month out. However, for the sake of this example, this person is doing everything but focusing on losing weight. Guess what? By the time their birthday rolls around, they are the same weight. They are disappointed. Other than writing it down or maybe saying it in their mind that initial time, they have given no more thought to losing weight.

The story's moral is that the goal must be relevant enough for the goal setter to maintain focus on achieving it. Instead of making a goal to lose weight in one month, another way to modify this goal and still accomplish it is to change the reason to be more relevant. Maybe losing weight to be healthier or reduce stress eating because it is building unhealthy habits is more pertinent. A consequence of reducing stress eating would be weight loss. Again, here's this quote: "You don't want to make a permanent decision based on temporary circumstances." Going through a stressful situation and being comforted by constant eating because it temporarily takes the mind off stressors results in weight gain. That weight will still be there and remain after the stressful situation has passed.

The T in SMART stands for **time-bound**. Again, using the example of becoming a millionaire, someone sets a goal and says, 'One day, I will become a millionaire.' Okay? So, one day means somewhere far off. How does one accomplish living out the vision far out? Is it going to be achieved in one month? Is it going to be completed in three months? Is it going to be performed in six months? Is it going to be met in two years? However long it takes, be realistic about achieving that goal. Put a timeframe on it to hold yourself accountable.

Now that you know what goes into setting a goal, let's talk about the daily steps or objectives. Short-term goals are even better than setting a long-term goal. Objectives can be accomplished in a shorter time and are often self-gratifying. Objectives even require less sacrifice to not exhaust oneself at the very outset. Once the goal is accomplished, people are often proud and feel more optimistic and are likely to set another goal because the last one was so easily accomplished.

Once you select the goal, you want to break it down. Let's get specific about this goal: 'I want to be a millionaire.' Does being a millionaire mean liquid cash? Does it mean going to the bank to withdraw cash on hand? Does it mean assets, meaning the value of all combined resources less what is owed? Or does being a millionaire mean owning assets free and clear will equal a million dollars?

Let's say you own a car. Well, cars depreciate. When a car is paid for, it's probably only worth about $8,000 to $10,000. That could be an asset. If it's free and clear, you own it and no longer pay a monthly car note. Let's say you own some investments. You have stock in different places. You have bonds, which you know are not worth that much unless you haven't touched them and have let them mature for decades. You are a homeowner. Well, now there is something that has some value because we know real estate appreciates over time. A car depreciates because you're driving it. It has issues. There's wear and tear. You'll need new tires and all these maintenance services.

Owning any real estate, even if you don't occupy it, is an investment. If you know someone who has owned a home for the past 20 years and you find out the purchase price, you may marvel at how much value they were able to get for their money 20 years ago. The amount paid for a house 20 years ago would be unimpressive in today's market. It is unimaginable in today's market to purchase a home for that low amount and expect duplicate square footage. Your following statement would be, if I could buy a house for that amount today, I'd be rich. You figure buying five or six properties at that price would make you a millionaire. Those were some common examples of how to define 'being a millionaire.'

After establishing the objectives, create daily steps. Let me give you an idea of how to set a goal for becoming a millionaire and make it a SMART goal. By December 31st, 2023, I will be a millionaire with one million dollars' worth of assets. That's a SMART goal. It's specific. Being a millionaire is measurable because I'm either a millionaire or not. It's achievable because the objectives will increase the probability of attaining them. It's relevant because becoming a millionaire means a lot to me. It's time-bound because I've given myself until December 31st, 2023, to achieve this goal.

Now for the objectives

Objective #1- I need to be mentored by someone who is already a millionaire.

Objective #2- I need to research Exchange-Traded Funds (EFT) because I want a diversified portfolio of stocks and bonds. I also need to research a trustworthy company to manage them.

Objective #3- I want to acquire three different types of real estate by the end of this year. *Now, specify what kind of real estate you wish to acquire.* I want to purchase an investment property for me to flip and resale. That means I'm going to buy the property. I'm going to rehab the rooms that need to be updated. I will put it back on the market to sell and profit from the house.

My second property may be real estate I can hold onto and occupy with renters. This may be a multi-unit apartment building. Now, I have a property that I will flip and make a quick profit. I have a property that I'm going to hold and fix up so it is habitable, and I can occupy it with renters.

The third property type may be Airbnb. I may purchase a single-family home to furnish and market as a vacation home. Another option for this furnished home would be to market it as corporate housing for employees who travel frequently. All these real estate ventures will contribute to my goal of becoming a millionaire.

Objective #4- Purchase a franchise. For this objective, I need to research different types of franchises or understand the top three revenue-generating industries in the country.

Once that is understood, figure out which turn-key business to start within that industry. Right now, the top three industries in the United States that have the most considerable revenue for 2022 are-

1. hospitals,
2. drug, cosmetic, and toiletry wholesaling industry (I'm sure the pandemic had a lot to do with this), and
3. new car dealerships.

Coming in close fourth place is life insurance and annuities. It would behoove me on my quest to become a millionaire to understand the drug cosmetic and toiletry wholesaling industry, understand and educate myself on new car dealerships, research and understand hospitals, and (I'm going to throw in four because it's just so good) understand life insurance and annuities.

Once that fundamental fact is considered, I can quickly increase my chances of becoming a millionaire. I've researched to identify that these are the top revenue-generating industries in the United States. I can get a portion of that revenue by owning a company in any of these areas (notice that I didn't say as an employee). I triple my chances of becoming a millionaire by the end of the year but to achieve this goal, I must put in daily objectives. Let me ask you a question, did that sound obtainable when establishing the goal to become a millionaire by the end of this year was first mentioned?

How many of you thought that goal was crazy? Nobody can go from zero to making a million dollars in just one year.

As I began to define how that could be accomplished and gave concrete objectives, the goal became more obtainable. It was easier to envision how it could be accomplished.

THE SCIENCE OF GOAL SETTING

The next very important step is mindset. You want to embody a healthy mindset so that you can see yourself accomplishing these goals. No one wants to set a goal or even begin trying to accomplish it if they don't feel that it's reachable. In most cases, people will feel defeated before they even start the goal, if the goal is too difficult to accomplish. When creating goals for yourself, make sure your mind believes you can accomplish them.

There's a science to setting goals. If you are setting goals that are easy to accomplish just because you don't want to fail, that's a huge problem. You are not challenging yourself. Please don't waste your own time setting goals that are easy to accomplish, especially if they never get you to that final goal. If it's too simple, you can achieve it without even setting a goal for it. To accomplish goals, some things will require you to be challenged, but the result will be so rewarding.

Education is another resource needed to achieve goals. Referencing the goal of becoming a millionaire in one year, it would benefit me to educate myself on EFTs and investment companies. I know nothing about EFTs, but they are popular now. Several people are using it to diversify their investments, and several people are having much success through trading on EFT apps. Sometimes, people do not seek out companies but trade on their own through these apps. I need to challenge myself and set a goal to learn more about EFTs (short-term goal/objective) for the greater purpose (long-term goal) of becoming a millionaire by the end of this year.

FAITH IS A MINDSET

You want to make sure that you can envision it and realize that it may take some work to accomplish the goal, but you are up for the challenge. It may take some time to achieve this goal, but you are committed. It would help if you were dedicated to seeing it through. That brings me to the next step: preparedness for the goal.

PREPAREDNESS FOR THE GOAL

How prepared are you? When you set objectives make sure that you prepare yourself. You must train your mind. You must organize your finances. You must encourage yourself to persevere beyond inevitable obstacles. You must dedicate time. Ask yourself, 'Will this take time away from me spending time with my family? Will I need to have some nights where I am going to ask my older children to be responsible for cooking or preparing dinner? Am I going to have to fix dinner ahead of time? Will I need to make food in the oven as opposed to having to cook something that requires a constant watch? Will I need to switch to easy prep meals that can self-cook by setting the oven to a timer?'

In being prepared, you may need to rearrange things. An example is not having to stand over the food, wait for it to simmer, boil, drain it, turn it over, and flip it. The example in the paragraph alleviates all this legwork. Accomplishing a goal will require creating a strategy. If you say that you don't have time, make time. If it normally takes you two and a half hours every evening to prepare and cook dinner, look up 30-minute, quick prep dinner recipes. Be willing to pivot and make changes. Save time by planning 30-minute meals for 30 days. Get back two hours per day and dedicate it towards achieving a goal. All these accommodations are ways to be more productive with time.

Take a moment to answer these questions. Write down the questions and answer them in your journal or on your phone or tablet.

How prepared are you to accomplish this goal?

Are you going to need resources?

Is this a goal that you cannot achieve on your own?

SPIRITUAL GOALS

What about a spiritual goal? Spiritual goals can be set as well. An example of this would be memorizing four scriptures a month. Certain scriptures come to mind as I encounter things in life, and I will often speak scriptures over my situation. I say it until I see my situation change. Maybe your spiritual goal is to read the Bible or pray every day for 30 minutes. Perhaps a spiritual goal is to prioritize spending time with God. An example of a goal would be to set aside the first 30 minutes of the morning to pray and listen to God for guidance and instruction. Another spiritual goal could involve checking emotions to think about good, positive, and virtuous things. This exhibits the fruit of the spirit- love, joy, peace, forbearance, kindness, goodness, faithfulness, gentleness, and self-control.

NO EXCUSES

I want to speak to your doubts for a minute. If I know most people, I know a certain number of people are reading this and thinking these steps can only be implemented in ideal situations. Some people feel that you don't have a tribe, a cheering corner, or anyone to hold you accountable.

When it comes to accountability, if you don't have people who can hold you accountable, hold yourself responsible. One way to do so is to set daily goals. Just take life one day at a time. View accomplishing a goal based on the daily effort that you put into it. If you know that you have accomplished something for the day, reward yourself for your effort.

Start by asking yourself, 'What can I do today to get myself closer to reaching the goal?' Do this daily. An example of daily things may be looking at EFTs. Downloading different apps that have daily notifications and teach information daily. This does not endorse these products, but Robinhood is an investment app. Another investment app is Webull.

Some apps help with time management and productivity. Go to the App Store or Google Play and search for goal setting or goal-tracking apps. There will be several apps that show in the list. There's another app called Focus, which helps you manage time to ensure you stay focused on your goal. There's another app called Pomodoro. This is good for setting goals and keeping you accountable. It includes a timer list. It has customizable settings that allow you to schedule your entire day. You can set intervals for work, schedule meetings, schedule time to pray, journal, etc. If you are considering applying for a grant, you can set the time to write for 10 minutes a day to dedicate towards writing a grant. You can set various reminders that make accountability work for you. If you don't want to download an app, the settings can be manipulated to notify your phone within a dedicated timeframe.

If the goal is to lose weight, there are apps for that. These apps can track what you eat, eating habits, the time of day you eat, how many calories you consume daily, and your activity levels. Again, there are several help aids for accountability.

CELEBRATE LIKE NOBODY'S BUSINESS

All work and no play is no fun. When you make goals, even your shortcomings bring you closer than where you were before you started. Make sure to reward yourself. Again, if you don't have a cheering corner, celebrate your successes alone.

Not every goal that you set will be accomplished. If the goal is incomplete, that's an opportunity for you to analyze the situation and see what needs to be adjusted. It doesn't mean that the goal will never be accomplished. Let's use the example of earning a million dollars or being a millionaire by the end of the year again. If that is too lofty of a goal and the goal is not reached because $300,000 was made by the end of the year instead of $1,000,000. Celebrate that! The goal wasn't met, but progress was made. Thirty percent of the goal was met, and that is worth celebrating! However long it takes, when that goal has been completed, celebrate like nobody's business! You've earned it, and you deserve it!

Self-care is a must. There won't be many things you can accomplish in general if you don't take the time to reward yourself. There will be a season in your life when things happen so quickly and easily that you must pinch yourself and ask, 'Is this my life right now? Are things happening this quickly for me?'

CHAPTER TEN

Write The Vision, Make It Plain

Now, it's time to recap everything we have explored in each chapter of this book to put it into action. I'm sure it may have taken several sittings to get to the end of this book. So that you don't have to flip back to the very beginning, a summary of each chapter is included below. This will be necessary to keep in mind the content that stood out to you as you read through this book. Use the prior information discussed along with prompts to write your vision.

In **Chapter ONE,** I shared my experience as a failed business owner and how it led to my purpose. I was able to heal from my pain and use it to lead people into their destinies and to encourage people to never stop pursuing their dreams. Think about a venture that you tried that may have been unsuccessful. Think about that time when things didn't turn out the way that you thought they would. It didn't go the way you envisioned. Now, think about what you must accomplish that requires you to step out on faith. How can you turn that frustration into motivation that will move you towards taking steps to manifest it?

Chapter TWO was designed to help you identify what inner qualities you possess. What qualities do you have that make other people admire you?

Is it your ambition? Is it your intellect? Is it your relatability? Is it your speaking voice? Is it your charisma? Is it your inner spirit? Is it how you command attention in a room full of people? Is it your writing skills?

What do you have within you that is natural for you, but other people struggle to do? What personality traits do you possess that others see and wish they had? Use that 'it' factor to create your unique recipe to set yourself apart from other people. This is also known as establishing your brand. Businesses often use this to set them apart from other businesses in the marketplace. What is your niche? This is part of what makes you unique and can be used to create your daily affirmations.

The goal of **Chapter THREE** was developed to get you to stop and assess where you are now and where you would like to go. The purpose of the tools was to help you answer your why. Why is it essential for you to get there? My pastor often says, 'So many people are connected to your destiny.' You must stay on track and fulfill your goals because you never know who is attached to your purpose. When you walk in your purpose, you are helping other people pursue their purpose.

In **Chapter FOUR**, we grappled with the idea of overcoming while becoming. You don't have to have it all together. You don't have to plan out every detail. You don't have to know how it will end before you take your first step. When you imagine things, you must be okay if real life deviates from that original idea. You must have flexibility. You must be pliable. You must be able to bend. You must be able to pivot.

If the 2020 pandemic we experienced over two years did not teach you anything else, it should have taught you that things happen that are out of your control. It would be best to think on your feet when things are out of your control. Be okay with change. Change doesn't have to be a complete change in direction. Is it alright if God wants to do something new within you? Is it okay if, while walking in your destiny, God also adds to it and finds other ways to bless you?

You may miss your blessing if you are stuck in your ways and not allowing God to do what He needs to do. The best way I can describe it is that God will crown your efforts with success. When God sees that you are working towards something, that act of faith will allow God to see you putting forth action. God will see it and add to it.

Overcoming while becoming means that we are all a work in progress. You have not arrived yet because you're still working on making improvements to get to where you want to be. In the process of getting to where you want to be, you will have several opportunities to get it right. If a test presents itself and you don't pass the test, the test will come around again.

Chapter FIVE began by asking, 'Where are you going?' Recognizing that your purpose can evolve as you gain new experiences, skills, and passions is essential. Don't be afraid to explore new opportunities and directions that align with your changing interests. Embrace the idea that your purpose can adapt and transform as you do.

Remember, fulfilling your purpose is both a responsibility and a privilege. It is up to you to actively seek and pursue it. Seek guidance from God, as He will provide direction and clarity along your journey.

Ultimately, the key is to stay open to the possibilities. Embrace your unique path and trust that it will lead you to where you are meant to be.

Your purpose is waiting to be discovered and fulfilled, and it is within your reach.

Chapter SIX started the self-help portion of the book. Being an overcomer means triumphing over challenges and obstacles, both external and internal. It requires being resolute, purposeful, and determined. You can overcome adversity by staying committed to your goals, learning from experiences, and appreciating personal growth. Remember, timelines or societal expectations do not define success. Surround yourself with supportive people and trust in your plan. Embrace challenges as opportunities for growth and persevere to create your life story.

Chapter SEVEN was a call to action to find a team of positive, encouraging, and genuine people. Create a list of positive people who have impacted your life in a good way and connect with them. Find people who celebrate others. Come together with a communicated vision for the well-being of humanity and move forward. Press on to become the unstoppable human being you were created to be!

Chapter EIGHT explored how to say what you want to see until it appears. Affirmations help make things a reality. Affirmations are spiritual. You can begin to use Biblical principles along with your affirmations. There's absolutely nothing wrong with adding the Word of God to your declarations. Please know that you can create statements on many areas in your life where you would like change to occur.

In **Chapter NINE**, we explored the steps required to set goals effectively. We began by emphasizing the importance of making goals obtainable and specific. We discussed SMART goals and how setting mini plans or objectives is crucial for progress. We stressed the importance of making goals measurable, achievable, relevant, and time bound. We also highlighted the significance of setting goals that are personally meaningful and rewarding.

Additionally, we provided sample goals. We explored how the right mindset is a prerequisite to starting something new. Finally, we touched on the importance of preparedness and making necessary adjustments to achieve goals effectively.

Now, let's write the vision.

Here are some prompts that can help you write a vision for your life:

1. What are your passions and interests? Consider what activities or topics make you feel vibrant and fulfilled.

2. What are your core values? Reflect on the principles and beliefs that guide your decisions and actions.

3. How do you envision your ideal lifestyle? Imagine how you would like to live your life regarding health, relationships (physical and spiritual), career, and personal growth.

4. What are your long-term goals and aspirations? Think about what you want to achieve: career, family, travel, or personal milestones.

5. What impact do you want to make in the world? Consider how you can contribute to society or make a difference in the lives of others.

6. How do you see yourself growing and evolving? Imagine the person you want to become and the skills, knowledge, or qualities you want to develop.

7. What legacy do you want to leave behind? Reflect on the mark you want to leave on the world and the lasting impact you want to have.

Remember, writing a vision is a personal and dynamic process. It's okay to revise and refine your vision as you grow and change.

CHAPTER ELEVEN

Take These with You

Are you ready to overcome? Are you ready to win? Hopefully, this book has made you think. I hope it's been motivating, reflective, and, most of all, encouraging. This is not a one-and-done book, meaning don't read through it and put it away. Use this book as a guide. Follow the chapters step by step and follow the recommendations in this book. Use the traits within you to make changes in your life.

What you don't possess, you can have access to by utilizing your resources. Resources don't only appear in the form of information on websites, libraries, or books. Resources show up through connections with people you know or introductions to people you may not know.

I want you to think about who you have in your life. Think about what you bring to the table. Then, think about the skills you want to develop to help you get to the next level. It would be pointless for you to have read this book and not act on any of the things mentioned. I have some takeaways that will sum up everything we've discussed and get you thinking in a way that will create results.

Takeaway number 1: A failure is just an experience where you fail forward. Failure does not have to be the end, especially when you use it as a learning experience to improve in the areas you lack sufficient skills. Use a failure or a failed venture, a failed connection, or a bad idea to improve. It is simply a learning lesson. It is not the end.

There is always an opportunity to grow in all things (good, bad, or indifferent). How you bounce back determines if you've taken advantage of turning a negative situation into a positive one. Remove the emotional sting of losing. Instead, gain retrospect to determine what you've gained from the situation. As a result of the failed venture, do you know what not to do the next time? As a result of the failed venture, did you learn who to contact for funding or sponsorship? As a result of the failed venture, did you attend networking events, and do you now have a collection of business cards or QR codes of new contacts for future prospective collaborations? Something good can come out of a bad situation. Sometimes, bad situations must occur to produce relentless character.

Takeaway number 2: You have gifts that are innately in your makeup. It is part of you. If you don't understand who you are, I encourage you to learn more about yourself and what makes you unique. What is that star quality that you have that no one else possesses? What is it about you that makes things happen when you walk into the room? Your life has a purpose.

Frequently, the area that was painful for you ends up being where you have the most purpose. You can relate to others' pain in that area because you've experienced it. You've been through some trials and tribulations. I encourage you to identify your gifts. Stop playing it safe and operate in excellence!

Takeaway number 3: If things continue to present themselves, it is an opportunity for you to do something different. Please do not continue to repeat the same self-sabotaging cycle. What is it about you that you keep getting attacked in a specific area? Take this subsequent trial as a test. Remove the emotional part of it. Look at it from an external perspective (as if you were outside looking into your situation). Pass the test.

You know how to self-assess if you have ever conducted a performance review on a direct report. What were your goals? Did you meet your goals within that quarter? What type of training do you need to complete those goals? Are you independent, or do you need to rely on management? What percent do you rely on management? What percent do you seek help when you have difficulty independently completing tasks? What other projects have you completed well that are outside of your scope of responsibilities? What overall rating would you give yourself? If you've answered all those questions, you've just completed a performance review. Use those answers to identify your strengths and weaknesses. Pass the test the next time around (wink).

Takeaway number 4: You are an overcomer. You are a conqueror. You are a winner. Winning takes strength, focus, and endurance. Most people who are overcomers don't win every battle, but they win the war. That takes strategy.

You may find it difficult to accept anything less, especially if you are an overachiever. However, stick to the plans. How do you eat an elephant? One bite at a time!

Takeaway number 5: Do not be afraid of a challenge. Do not become defeated without ever giving it a try. If the only opportunities that you want are the ones that come quickly, then that is not a challenge. Everything easy is not meant for you. Anything worth having is worth working for. Be willing to put forth the effort. What is your motivation? What drives you? Think about that and keep that front and center when pursuing your passions.

God always has a plan. God will make provisions for you so things don't become too complicated. You have no idea what He has already shielded you from. God is a protector, a warrior, and a mighty King!

Takeaway number 6: Don't let your gift take you where your character can't keep you. At all times, it is so important to realize that even the gifts that you display are not simply just for you. Winning and overcoming is a win for the next person. Others are motivated by you and can take a page from your success book. You never know who's watching you. You never know who you encourage by never speaking a word. Your actions are being watched.

Takeaway number 7: Be confident. Be resolute. Be steadfast. Be immovable. Be able to handle things from the perspective of EI. Understand what qualities you possess that make you relate to people. Understand that having a positive outlook on life is a strength. What are those traits and qualities that you possess? How can you respond to life's challenges?

How should you respond to something out of your control while maintaining control over your emotions? Cry. After 24 hours, let it go. Fall, but always get back up. Pray, fully expecting your prayers to be answered.

Takeaway number 8: If you fail to plan, then you plan to fail. It is impossible to be an overcomer without planning. Let setting goals and creating to-do lists be your guide. Checklists, questionnaires, and accountability are ways to ensure everything is in order. Celebrate each completed task. Celebrate each achieved goal. Celebrate each win. It will give you the momentum that you need to keep going.

Before engaging in any goal setting, set your mind. The worst thing that you can do is negative self-talk. Yes, you can do it! Yes, it can be you! Yes, you will achieve it! Yes, God has favored you!

Takeaway number 9:

1. Do the work.
2. Write out your affirmations.
3. Speak the affirmations daily.
4. Back them with scripture.

Most affirmations come from the Bible. There is a scripture for everything that you face in life. There is nothing new under the sun.

Faith without works is dead. You are past the planning phase. When building a house, you start with a blueprint. After creating the drawing, you hire a team who gets the materials. After they gather the materials, they get to work! They start with the foundation of the house. They frame the house on the inside. They put up support beams. They build the basement, the main level, and the top floor. After finishing the framework on the inside, they assemble the roof. Don't be so worried about your roof (your outer appearance) that you forget to build the framework (your inner self). It would be a shame to have gone through all the inner work and never have faith to put on the top layer (roof). Stop starting and stopping. It is time to finish strong!

Takeaway number 10: You are too brilliant to not be a millionaire. Understand that you are unique. You are great. You are wonderful. You are generous. You are loving. You are multifaceted. You are all these things in one, yet no one else is like you. Even if you are a twin, you are unique.

My entire life has been built on helping people. I am a speech-language pathologist. I am a mother of five. I am a wife. I am a research manager. I am a doctor of Speech-Language Pathology. I am a business owner. I am a helper. I am an edifier. I understand that those are my spiritual gifts. Helping people is my purpose, and that manifests itself in several ways. These are all the ways my gifts manifest.

To summarize this book, it is enough work to focus on what you want from life. How dare you be here, breathing air, taking up space, and not getting what you desire out of life? You don't have to do it alone. God sends people into your life. If any of this speaks to you, I encourage you to contact me on social media and let's get together to see how I can help you. You can enroll in my 'Take Action' course to begin to live your hero story!

Acknowledgments

I would like to take this opportunity to thank God for being faithful and for seeing me through the completion of yet another personal goal. God is faithful! I acknowledge that many of my experiences, though sometimes painful, had a purpose and were necessary for growth. Without those trials and victories, I would not have the wisdom to share with others. I would not be able to walk in what God purposed for my life. Father, I am eternally grateful for that!

My husband and five wonderful children are my core. Kevon, thank you for being my life partner and confidant. Your role in helping me develop this book has been so crucial. I know that you want the very best for me and I thank you for helping me push past mental blocks. You have contributed to this work in a major way. My wonderful children are my world!!! In everything that I do, I hope to be an example for all of you (Shania, Kevon Jr., Kyle, Kennedi, and Kaleb).

A huge thank you to Dr. Sherrie Walton, the best book coach on this side of heaven. Thank you for challenging me to release everything within me. Some of these stories were from years ago. Revisiting them brought back several emotions and I was in that place all over again. Only this time it was from a place of peace and strength. When I thought I had said it all, you found more ways for me to tell my story using a different perspective!

Thank you for your patience and for holding me accountable. I thank God for you!

To my extended family, many of the stories that I share in this book involve you. Thank you for holding me down, for being by my side, and for journeying through life with me. You've allowed me to see myself through your eyes. You provided a shoulder when I needed to cry, an ear when I needed to vent, advice when I needed guidance, laughter when I needed to be uplifted, and a loving push when I wanted to give up. You've seen me at my most vulnerable times. You've interceded for me, and your prayers reached heaven's gates! Thank you from the bottom of my heart.

About The Author

D r. Shawnise Carter is a highly experienced and dedicated professional in the field of speech-language pathology. With an impressive 18 years of treating, mentoring, supervising, and conducting research, she has established herself as a leading authority in her field. Dr. Carter's educational background is equally impressive, having earned her bachelor's and master's degrees in speech and hearing sciences from Tennessee State University, as well as her Doctor of Science degree in speech-language pathology from Rocky Mountain University of Health Professions.

Currently, Dr. Carter utilizes her vast knowledge and expertise to enhance the development of innovative speech-language pathology products. She actively contributes to the field by serving as a board member for various organizations. Her dedication to academic research is evident through her involvement as a committee chair for doctoral students. Beyond her professional responsibilities, Dr. Carter is the owner of a personal care agency.

Dr. Carter's passion for her work is undeniable, as she continuously seeks opportunities to make a positive impact on the lives of aspiring business owners as well as individuals with communication disorders. She speaks on various panels involving entrepreneurship. With her friendly demeanor and creative problem-solving skills, she is not only a respected professional but also a reliable and compassionate resource for those seeking guidance in business ownership. Her professional speaking engagements often inform her audience of ways to leverage their combined skills to create unconventional income streams.

Follow Dr. Carter on Instgram- @drshawmazing

Stay in the know with the latest book signings by following her on social media and by visiting her website often- www.drshawmazing.com.

Follow her business FaceBook page- SC Collabs

If you are interested in taking her My Hero Story course to optimize your own personal growth journey, register at www.drshawmazing.com/course

If you are interested being coached by Dr. Carter to learn how to increase revenue by packaging your skills in ways that gain you consultative work, please email: bookme@drshawmazing.com or inbox her on any of her social media pages.

If you are interested in booking her for media, podcasts, or speaking engagements, please email: bookme@drshawmazing.com.

Go be brilliant!